Walking in the Hambleton Hills

By

Keven Shevels

TRAIL GUIDES publications

First published in Great Britain in 2015 by Trailguides Limited.
www.trailguides.co.uk

ISBN 978-1-905444-60-1

The route diagrams in this book are based upon 1925-1940 Ordnance Survey One-Inch maps updated by field trips and site visits.

Trailguides Limited
35 Carmel Road South
Darlington
Co Durham DL3 8DQ

Cover design by Steve Gustard
Artwork by Trailguides Limited

CONTENTS

Cover photos.
Front. Heading towards Studfold. Walk 8 Studfold and Pry Rigg Plantation. Back cover. Looking across Arden Great Moor. Walk 6 Arden Great Moor.

INTRODUCTION

1. Introduction

The Hambleton Hills are a range of hills that run for about fifteen miles along the western edge of the North York Moors. They also form the eastern boundary of the low-lying Vale of Mowbray which they join via a steep escarpment which in many places forms a sheer cliff edge. Running in a north-south direction, they merge in the north with the rugged Cleveland Hills while in the south they flow down to join the more gentle, rolling Howardian Hills. To the east, the valley of the River Rye separates them from the main bulk of the Moors and the Tabular Hills, which form the southern edge of this upland.

In terms of size, this is a fairly small area of land but one that is very varied. To the north sits Black Hambleton, at 380 metres (1,247 feet) the highest point in these hills. Here the Hambletons are a wide open expanse of heather moorland and during summer, awash with the colour purple from the flowering plants. As the hills run towards the south, the landscape becomes more cultivated with first grazing for sheep and then as you get further south, the fields start to fill with crops. The hills themselves are relatively flat-topped and while the western edge is a steep-sided escarpment, to the east small, narrow valleys cut into the side of the hills and run down to the River Rye. On both the east and west, the sides of the hills are clothed in woods and plantations giving a green border that outlines the hills.

Man has settled on these hills since the earliest of times. Evidence of the Neolithic, Bronze Age and Iron Age lie in many places across the hill tops showing how man has changed the landscape to suit himself. Then as civilisation developed, these hills became the setting for conflict and worship plus many things in-between. All of which, leaving tell-tale marks across this countryside.

For the walker, the mix of the varied landscape and the long history of these hills presents a fascinating backdrop to a number of very pleasant days out in a countryside that deserves to be walked.

2. Access & the Right to Roam

To the south, the Hambleton Hills consist of a mixture of farmland and woods. Here access is generally restricted to public rights of way, in the main footpaths and bridleways, and the walks in this book that cross that part of the hills reflect this. However, in the north, once you are on the heather moors then access becomes more flexible. The North York Moors are the largest expanse of heather moorland in the country and, as a result, a prime grouse shooting area and in the past access to these moors has been jealously guarded in order to protect the game birds. As a result walkers have been restricted to public rights of way. A policy which has, in many ways, prevented the responsible walker from experiencing some of the best of the moors.

With the implementation of the Countryside Right of Way Act 2000 in 2005 and the introduction of the "Right to Roam" this has changed some of the access rights and certain upland areas of the Moors have now become legally accessible away from public rights of way. This legislation allows walkers the right to roam at will over “designated access land” without the need to be restricted to official footpaths and bridleways.

On the new editions of the Ordnance Survey Explorer maps, this new access land is marked with a light yellow coloured background and at the entry points to this land, the stiles and gates carry the new “access land” waymarking symbol of a brown stick man in a brown circle. The details that accompany each of the walk descriptions will provide information as to whether the route uses rights of way or crosses open access land.

With the right to access has also come responsibility and the walker is expected to observe various limits and restrictions that are placed on their activities at certain times of the year. The landowner and/or farmer has the right to exclude access for up to twenty eight days per year and this is normally applied between May and early July to coincide with the breeding season of the ground-nesting birds on the moors. Where they are known, restrictions that may impinge on any given walk are shown in the details for that walk. However, don't take it for granted that these are going to be accurate as in each year these restrictions may change. Always check any notices that are placed at the access points for any restrictions. To find out more about the `right to roam` and whether any general or specific restrictions apply to any part of the North York Moors then a visit to the website www.countrysideaccess.gov.uk will give you all the necessary information.

3. The Walks

The nine walks in this book have all been designed to explore the countryside of the Hambleton Hills, a varied countryside of fields, hills, moors and woods. The walks chosen showcase both the variety of the landscape and also the history of this part of the North York Moors. The walks start from a number of different locations around the Hills with the starting location and its grid reference being given within the introductory details of that walk.

Anybody who has used one of my books before will realise that I have a little bit of a passion for history and how this is reflected in the landscape. As always, this is shown within these walks as I quite frequently use them to visit and explore certain aspects of the countryside that I, personally, find quite interesting. I don't believe that walking guidebooks should be boring and, hopefully, the walks and associated notes will help convey my enthusiasm for the landscape of the North York Moors to you, both as a reader and as a walker.

In the details preceding each of the walks there is an approximate time taken for that particular walk which includes a reasonable time to explore the various sites of interest that are visited. However, this can be variable depending upon how long you, as the walker, take to explore these sites. If you chose not to have a look and investigate then the time taken will obviously be shorter whereas if you linger and have a good mooch about then you may be longer than I have estimated.

The walks in this book have all been graded in accordance with the Ferguson Grading System (`FGS`) and the actual grading is set out at the beginning of each individual walk to help you assess their difficulty. A detailed explanation of the FGS and how individual gradings are determined is set out on pages 107-109 in the Appendix to this book.

4. The Weather

Although the Hambleton Hills, are not particularly high in comparison to the Pennines or the Lakeland fells, as part of the North York Moors they are still high, open countryside whether it is the fields of the southern end of the Hills or the moors of the northern part and as such are susceptible to sudden changes in weather which can present a risk for those walkers who are inadequately prepared.

In summer, when the sun beats down, this open rolling landscape can present very little shade. Therefore, in hot weather you should always carry sufficient fluid or drinks to avoid the risk of dehydration and if prone to the heat or sunburn, wear a hat and/or sunblock. In contrast, this same open landscape can offer little shelter from both wind and rain and bad weather can sweep across these hills with little warning. If rain comes, then this is often accompanied by a drop in temperature and even in high summer, localised hail and snow are not unknown. In the autumn and winter months, fog and mist are also a real possibility although the surprising factor here is that it can quite often come from the low-lying Vales of Mowbray and York to the west, creeping along the valleys on the edge of the escarpment and up to the hills. Looking at a map will show the position of the North York Moors as being adjacent to the North Sea. In most winters this usually makes them one of the first places to see snow in the North East.

Even on these low hills, it is important to be properly equipped when venturing out across this countryside.

5. The Maps

The Hambleton Hills lie to the south west of the North York Moors, running north to south along the western escarpment. Only the one map is required for all the walks in this book and that is Ordnance Survey OL 26 North York Moors Western area.

The route descriptions included in this book are meant as a guide and although under normal conditions they should be sufficient to guide you round the route, they are not intended to replace the use of the relevant map. Nor is the sketch diagram of the route meant to replace the OS map but rather to be used as an aid for you to identify the route on the map.

Although not particularly high, this countryside can be wild and rough, which is part of its attraction, and the weather can be very changeable. It is quite possible to set off in brilliant sunshine and then to find that later, low cloud and rain has come rolling in and visibility is very poor. The ability to navigate with map and compass is a required skill to safely traverse these hills and it would be extremely foolhardy to venture out with just this guidebook and no map.

6. Facilities, Tourist Information Centres & Websites

On both the western and southern edges of the hills are a number of small villages, which are shown on the Walk Location Map. Most of these, but not all, have public houses which can offer refreshments including food and in some cases accommodation. The larger villages, such as Kilburn and Osmotherley, are popular tourist locations in their own right and are also able to offer cafes and village shops.

These villages can also provide accommodation ranging from bed and breakfast, self-catering cottages and hotel rooms. An enquiry to the tourist information centres below or a quick search on the internet will provide more details.

Within the Hambleton Hills themselves, there are no tourist information centres but a short distance away, on the western edge of the hills, the towns of Northallerton and Thirsk both boast centres. The details of these are below and both centres cover the small villages along the western side of the escarpment.

Northallerton Tourist Information Centre.
The Applegarth Car Park, Northallerton. North Yorkshire. DL7 8LZ.

Telephone. 01609 776864

Thirsk Tourist Information Centre.
93A Market Place. Thirsk. North Yorkshire. YO7 1EY.
Telephone. 01845 522755

In addition to these two offices, the North York Moors National Park operate a visitor centre located at the top of Sutton Bank, on the A170 Thirsk to Helmsley road. This is a sizeable centre complete with café, displays on the national park, shop, and bike shop. There are also a number of waymarked trails starting from here plus parking and outside picnic areas.

Sutton Bank National Park Centre
Sutton Bank. Thirsk. North Yorkshire. Y07 2EH
Tel. 01845 597426
Email. suttonbank@northyorkmoors.org.uk

Being part of the North York Moors National Park, the area is covered by the Park's website which contains news about the park as well as providing advice and articles on events within the park, where to visit, facilities including accommodation, and many other things that this wonderful area has to offer. The website can be accessed at **www.northyorkmoors.org.uk**.

WALK LOCATION MAP

Location of start of walk number.

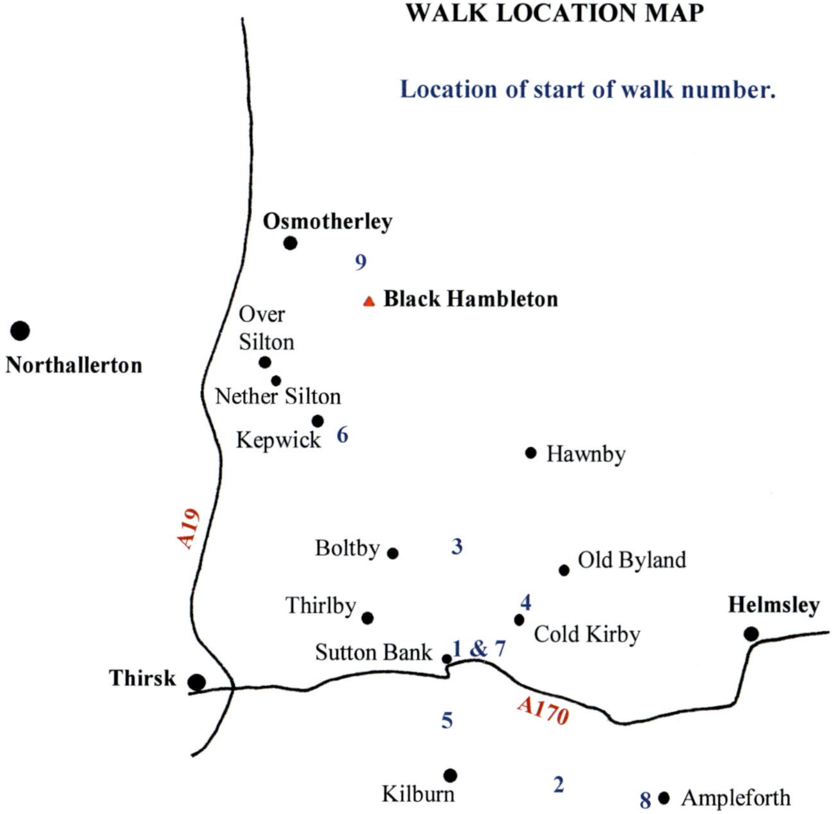

The view towards Hood Hill from Sutton Bank.

The view from Roulston Scar towards the end of the walk and, inset, heading up the lane towards High Town Brow. Walk 1: Scotch Corner and Roulston Scar.

WALK 1: SCOTCH CORNER AND ROULSTON SCAR.

Not the longest walk in the book but one that is full of interest not least because, if they are flying, you have the opportunity to watch the gliders from the Yorkshire Gliding Club soaring on the thermals above Sutton Bank. However, that fascination aside, on this walk you can tread in the footsteps of our prehistoric ancestors, imagine the screams and shouts of men as they killed and died in a battle between the English and Scots during the Middle-Ages, admire the handiwork of an acclaimed sculptor as he honoured the fallen of another, much later conflict and finally, come up close and personal with one of the region's most well-known landmarks.

DISTANCE: 6.1 miles / 9.8 km.
ASCENT: 715 feet / 218 metres.
TERRAIN: The route is mainly along well-surfaced path and track with a couple of sections of quiet country lane thrown in. There is one short section through the woods leading to the Yorkshire Gliding Club's airfield that may be a bit soft and boggy after wet weather. There is one long descent leading down from the top of the Moors to the outskirts of the village of Oldstead and conversely there is one long slog up High Town Brow as you make your way back to the top of the Moors.
START: The North York Moors National Park visitor centre at the top of Sutton Bank. GR SE 516 831.
TIME: 3½ to 4 hours.
ACCESS: The route is all on public rights of way.
DOGS: As the route is all on rights of way then dogs are allowed. However, you may want to keep them on a lead as you walk round the edge of the escarpment on the return leg. You are unlikely to meet livestock on this walk but you are quite likely to meet other dogs as you come back along Roulston Scar.

GRID REFERENCES.

Sutton Bank visitor centre	516 831
Path junction	517 826
Path/road junction	521 829
Road/track junction	521 822
Scotch Corner	530 811
Lane/road junction	530 805
Road/lane junction	523 805
Lane/path junction	521 816

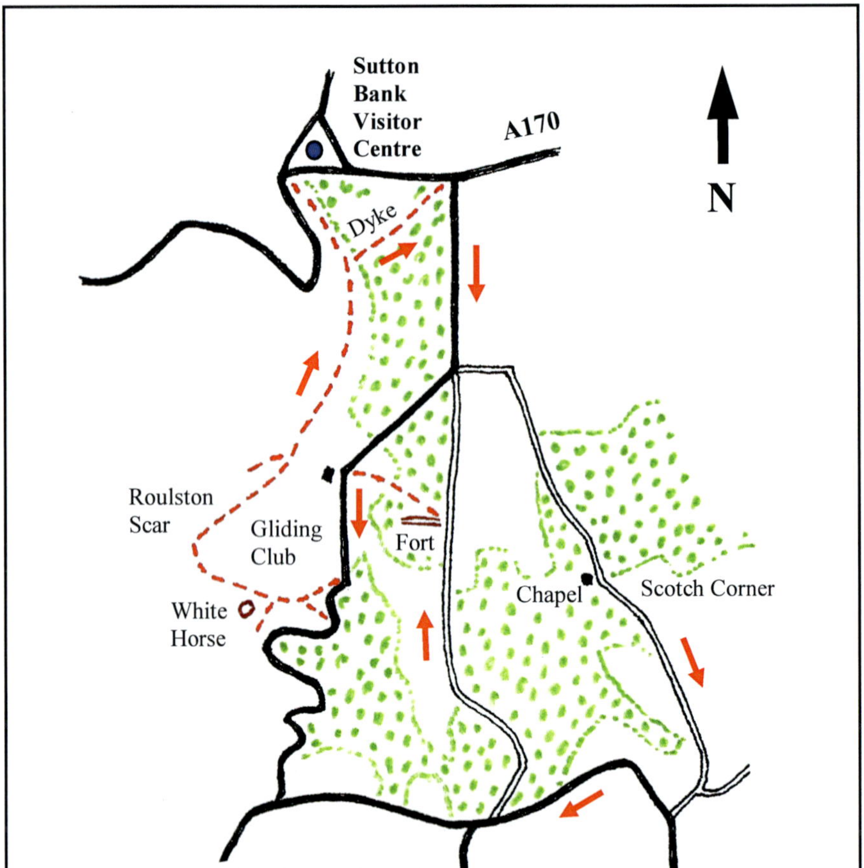

Below, crossing the A170 at the start of the walk and, right, the memorial stone to lost airmen.

Path/road junction	517 818
Road/path junction	517 815
Path junction	514 813
Sutton Bank visitor centre	516 831

FGS GRADING

Grading is T4 [D1, N1, T0, R1, H1]

Distance	**1**	6 – 12 miles
Navigation	**1**	Basic navigation skills needed
Terrain	**0**	75% + on graded track or path
Remoteness	**1**	Countryside in fairly close proximity to habitation – at least 80% of the route within 2 miles
Height	**1**	Over 100 ft per mile

THE WALK

1. From the car park at the visitor centre, make your way through the grounds of the visitor centre to the top of Sutton Bank. Once here cross the A170 to the southern side of the road to a Cleveland Way signpost stating that the White Horse is 1 mile away.

Follow the path to the White Horse and after a couple of metres come to a junction. Bear left and within a short distance come to a second junction where you bear left again and follow the path along the edge of the escarpment.

The path passes a small memorial stone to lost airmen and then comes to a junction with a path on the left marked by a Cleveland Way signpost with the narrative 'Hambleton A170' on it. As you approach, the signpost is partially hidden by trees. **GR 517 826.**

2. Turn left here and follow the path as it heads away from the escarpment edge. Running on the left-hand side of the path is the Castern Dike. After a little while the path comes to a road junction. **GR 521 829.**

Shown on the map as the Castern Dike, the ditch and bank that runs alongside the left of the path is part of the Cleave Dyke system of earthworks that cover a large area of the southern Hambleton Hills. Many of the dykes run parallel with and close to the western edge of the hills while others run at 90 degrees, cutting across the hill top to the eastern side. Built at some point between the late Bronze Age and the Iron Age, around 3,000 years ago, the system is a complex of linear ditches and banks that was constructed to enhance the natural division of the terrain by the river valleys and watersheds and forms a sequence of territorial boundaries. In an area that was mainly given over to the grazing of livestock, these earthworks must have been an impressive symbol for their builders. In an age when tribal prestige was all important, the message that 'we are here, we are important and we can build these' was screamed long and loud. Although worn by 3,000 years of erosion and destruction by subsequent generations, significant stretches of the dyke system remain as standing earthworks all across these hills and more can be seen as crop marks on aerial photographs.

3. Turn right to follow the minor road, signposted 'Yorkshire Gliding Club and White Horse', for 700 metres until you come to a point where the road turns right and there is a track going straight ahead and a second track going to the left. **GR 521 822.**

4. Here, leave the road to turn left and follow the track for a short distance to come to a corner and then follow the main track as it turns to the right. Continue along the track and after a little while it does a little kink to the left to enter a wood.

Stay on the track to come to a crossroads where you continue straight ahead. Eventually the track starts to descend and then bends to the right. Here, ignore the second track that comes in on the left to follow the main track round to the right and pass the buildings of the John Bunting Memorial Chapel.

The small building on the corner of the track in this lonely part of the Hambleton Hills is a chapel erected in remembrance to those who died during the Second World War. The work of acclaimed sculptor John Bunting, it is built on the ruins of an old farmstead and is home to many of his works including a stone sculpture of a recumbent soldier in paratrooper's helmet and commando boots. A statue of a mother and child sits a few metres away, above the chapel. The land on which it sits was acquired in 1956 and the chapel rebuilt over the following years and is now managed by the Bunting family for the public benefit. Over the last couple of years, the Bunting family and the National Park Authority have worked together to open the chapel to the public on selected days. More information on John Bunting and his chapel can be obtained from the information boards outside the building.

John Bunting's Chapel and, top right, the carved detail above the door and, bottom right, the mother and child figure in the grounds.

Continue downhill on the track. Towards the bottom of the bank, pass another track on the left and continue straight ahead to leave the woods as the track now goes between fields. Within a hundred metres or so, you'll come to an information board on the Exmoor ponies in the fields on the right of the track and just after that a gate and a footpath marker on the left. This point on the route is shown on the map as Scotch Corner, site of a battle between the English and the Scots. **GR 530 811.**

BATTLE OF SCOTCH CORNER

October 14, 1322 and the quiet peace of this isolated hill above Oldstead is riven by the shouts and screams of those killing and those dying. It is during the First War of Scottish Independence and Robert Bruce, King of Scotland, had invaded northern England burning and plundering as he made his way south. The English army under Edward II, an unpopular and weak king, had already lost 20,000 men mainly through disease, hunger and ineptitude, fled south before the Scots and found refuge in the Hambleton Hills. While the English were waiting for reinforcements, the Scots located the remnants of their army and launched a devastating attack. Initially the English held their own, they held the high ground and were able to fire down on the attacking Scots as they struggled up the steep slopes towards them. However, in a flanking move a detachment of Scottish troops had made their way up the side of the hill and then descended on the English below. More ineffectual leadership meant that the English had not defended their rear, already demoralised and now panic stricken they broke before the determined Scottish attack and were slaughtered. Rather than die with his men, Edward fled for his life riding non-stop to Bridlington and safety. At liberty to do as they wished, the Scots then sacked the nearby abbeys of Byland and Rievaulx before heading for York. And so ended the Battle of Scotch Corner, or Battle of Byland as it is sometimes known. A humiliating defeat for the English.

As you stand here looking over the field and the wind blows through the trees, ask yourself, is that really the wind ....

The ridge of Scotch Corner, scene of a bloody battle between the English and Scots.

5. Continue to follow the track downhill. The descent does become a bit steeper but when you do finally get to the bottom of the bank you join a tarmac lane that comes in from the left. Here continue straight ahead along the lane for a couple of hundred metres to join the side of a road. **GR 530 805.**

6. Turn right to follow the road. After about 300 metres the road bends to the left and after a further 600 metres comes to a tarmac lane on the right side of the road. The entrance to the lane is marked by signs for the 656 cycleway route and a large 'Unsuitable for motor vehicles' sign and is about 30 metres in front of a junction with another road coming in on the left. **GR 523 805.**

7. Here, turn right to follow the lane uphill, passing a small BT building on the left of the lane. The lane climbs quite steeply up through the woods until it bends to the left and then the gradient eases off slightly although there is still a long and steady climb to make as the lane continues up High Town Brow.

Eventually the lane leaves the woods although this may be difficult to tell as there are still trees and bushes lining the side of it. When you do finally get to the top of the bank, the lane passes a track on the left that goes into a field and another wood starts on the left hand side.

Continue for another 200 metres to come to a well-used path that leaves the left-side of the lane . There is no signpost marking the path but there is a metal gate opposite on the right-side of the lane that helps identify it. The path did once go off into the trees of the wood but now the trees on the right of the path have been felled. However, those on the left still stand and so the path now runs along the edge of them. **GR 521 816.**

Before you leave the road have a look at a slight bank on the left of the path, just within the trees. These are the remains of Roulston Scar Hill Fort.

8. Leave the lane to turn left and follow the path along the edge of the trees. After a while you'll come to a path junction with a marker post just in front of you. Continue on the path straight ahead as it now starts to go between the trees.

After a little while you'll come to another marker post and here the path bends to the left. However, don't follow it, instead go straight ahead to join the road, which is less than 100 metres away, in front of the buildings of the Yorkshire Gliding Club. **GR 517 818.**

Located at Sutton Bank since the 1930's, the Yorkshire Gliding Club is one of the leading clubs in the country. As you walk past it, the most obvious feature, apart from the flat grassy landing field, is the circular clubhouse that was built in the 1960's. The route of the walk now follows the edge of the escarpment as it goes round Roulston Scar, travelling from one side of the landing field to the other and, if flying conditions are favourable, giving excellent views of the gliders as they take advantage of the thermals that rise from the cliff walls.

9. Turn left to follow the road as it follows the side of the airfield. After a couple of hundred metres, you'll come to a couple of car parks either side of the road, just before the road starts to descend quite steeply. **GR 517 815.**

10. Here turn right to leave the road and go to a visible footpath marker post that marks the start of a gravel path. Follow the path as at first it shadows the road and then bends to the right to cross a footbridge and head away from the road, going round the front of the escarpment. After several hundred metres you'll come to a path junction that stands at the top of the Kilburn White Horse. **GR 514 813.**

11. Continue straight ahead as the path follows the edge of the escarpment giving exceptional views out over the Vale of Mowbray and passes a number of information boards.

Eventually the path comes to the point where you turned away from the edge of the escarpment at the start of the walk, passes the memorial stone to the lost airmen and arrives back at the side of the A170. Taking care, cross the road and return back to the visitor centre.

ROULSTON SCAR HILL FORT

Although not looking much more than an earthen bank running between the trees, this bank actually forms part of the defences of the Roulston Scar Hill Fort. This fort, which was re-examined in 2001, is a huge complex, more than twice the size of most other hill forts in the region and making it the largest of its kind in the north of England. Covering more than 60 acres (24 hectares) including most of the land taken up by the Yorkshire Gliding Club, the fort is situated on Roulston Scar and High Town Brow in an outstanding defensive position. Built of timber palisades and with a 1.3 mile (2.1 km) circuit of ramparts, 60 per cent of which are cut out of solid limestone, the defences circled the entire promontory and allowed two individual plateaus to be defended. Being such a large structure, the fort would have taken several years to build and would have needed at least 10,000 cubic metres of earth and rock plus more than 3,000 trees. The fort has been provisionally dated at 400 BC.

The earth bank running through the trees.

The site occupies a naturally strong position, defended to the west by a cliff face, to the south by a steep slope, and on the east side by a steep-sided valley known as Boar's Gill. From this position, it commands breath-taking views over the Vales of Mowbray and York. The neck of land to the north was defended by over 300 metres of box rampart, which had survived as a bank up to 8 metres wide and 3 metres high with a broad ditch silted up to 0.9 metre deep and a low counterscarp bank. This was continued around the other sides of the promontory by a glacis rampart up to 2.5 metres high, again with a low counterscarp bank. Unfortunately most of the box rampart was levelled during the 1970's when the runway for the gliding club was extended. Most of the other ramparts have been fairly well preserved, however, here on the south-east side they have been damaged by the forestation but are still identifiable as a sizeable earthwork. Over on the southern side of the promontory, around the Kilburn White Horse, the banks and ditches are still visible although part of them were cut through in 1857 by the head of the Horse when it was constructed.

Because of the landing field extension, there are no clear traces on the ground surface that the fort was occupied, any that were here will have been removed when the land was graded during the 1960's. However, to the eastern side of the fort in a quarry hollow, there are signs that there may have been house platforms immediately behind the eastern rampart.

Leaving the road after passing the gliding club, the gravel path crosses a bridge over one of the ditches of the earthworks. Below right, the ditch continuing on from the bridge. Below left, one of the low earth walls to the right of the gravel path as you approach the White Horse.

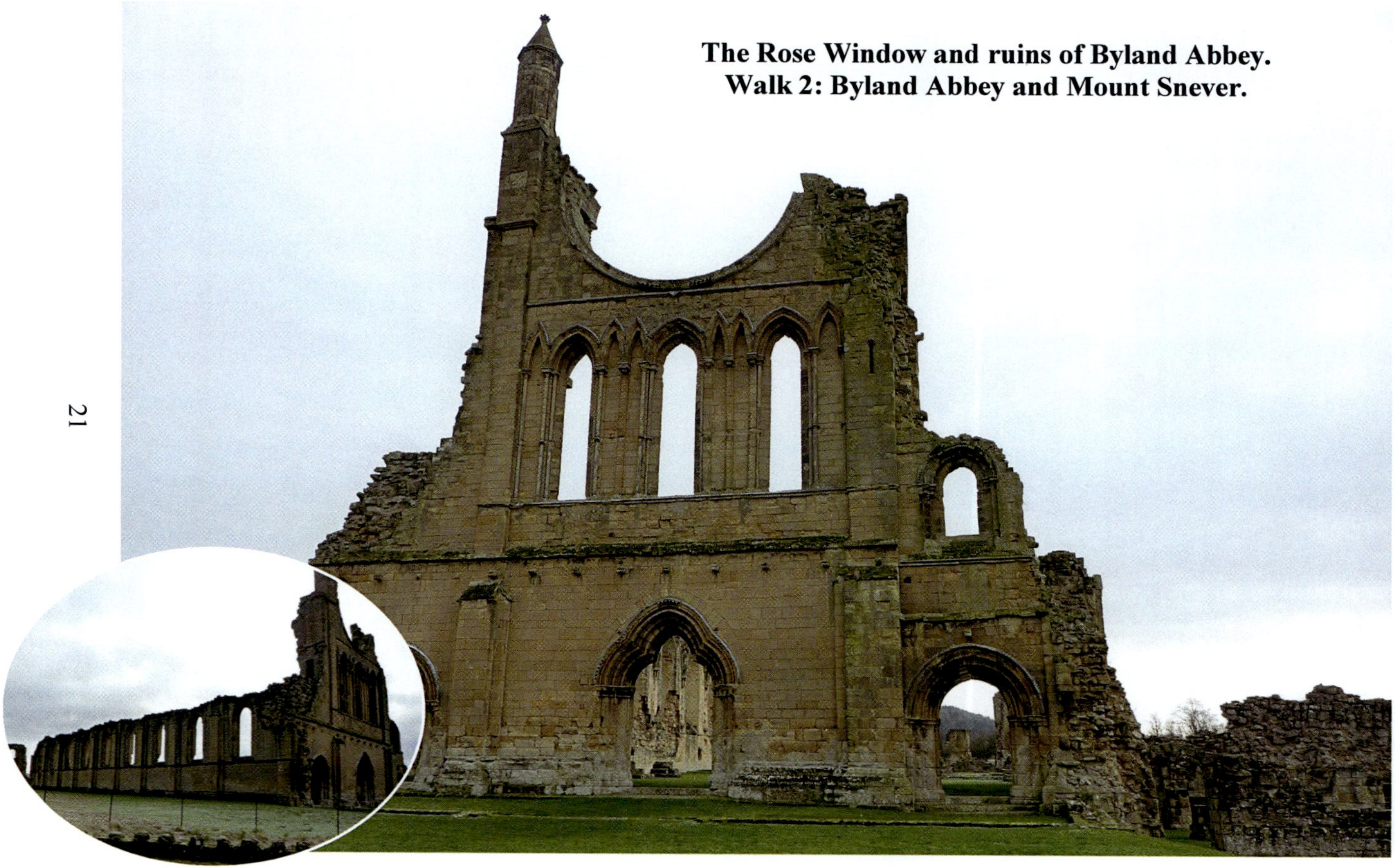

The Rose Window and ruins of Byland Abbey.
Walk 2: Byland Abbey and Mount Snever.

BYLAND ABBEY

The ruins at Byland Abbey are dominated by the remains of the great rose window, a structure that inspired the design of the world-famous rose window of York Minster. Although in ruins now, the abbey was one of the greatest monasteries in England and its early Gothic architecture was an inspiration for church buildings throughout the north.

Founded by the Savigniac order of monks under the patronage of Roger de Mowbray, one of the richest landowners in England, construction started around 1155. The next twenty years were spent clearing the wild and marshy ground, draining the land, and preparing the site ready for the building of the abbey. By 1177 sufficient buildings had been completed so that the monks could begin to occupy the site. However, the construction of the great church would take another fifteen years before completion.

Due to the generosity of a number of benefactors, especially Roger de Mowbray, a considerable estate was built-up by the abbey. This was farmed by the lay-brothers and servants of the abbey. To the east, the main holdings went beyond Ampleforth and Thorpe, while to the west they went to Sutton-under-Whitestonecliffe and Marderby. In addition there were holdings in other parts of the country, in particular Cumbria, with granges at Asby, Warcop, and Bleatarn. Although never as wealthy as neighbouring Rievaulx, the abbey at Byland was far from poor.

However, by the end of the 14th century Byland had suffered a number of hardships. In 1322, after the Battle of Scotch Corner, the victorious Scots army looted the abbey taking away a considerable amount of booty. The same century brought the Black Death, along with the rest of England, the monks and lay-population of the abbey was decimated. No longer having sufficient manpower to work the estates, the abbey's ability to generate income was severely curtailed.

In time, Byland slowly started to regain its position but then Henry VIII had his falling out with the Church of Rome. In 1538 Byland surrendered to the dissolution and the wealth of the abbey was taken by the Crown. This included the wealth of the buildings themselves which were stripped of all lead, glass, and fixtures. By the time that the abbey was granted to Sir William Pickering in 1540, the buildings were starting to become ruins with the stonework being stripped and used in local buildings.

The abbey is now owned by the Newburgh Estate and managed by English Heritage.

WALK 2: BYLAND ABBEY AND MOUNT SNEVER

A walk to the south-east of Sutton Bank that starts just outside Byland Abbey and gives the opportunity to visit the ruins of this, one of the most significant religious houses in the north of England during the medieval period. Sadly, as with most medieval abbeys, the place is now a ruin but still impressive, especially the frame of the circular Rose Window which was the inspiration of the famous Rose Window in York Minster.

DISTANCE: 6.1 miles / 9.8 km.
ASCENT: 801 feet / 244 metres.
TERRAIN: A mixture of field and woodland paths and tracks. In winter and wet weather, some of these paths may be quite muddy. There are a couple of short road sections on this walk. There is a little bit of a steep climb up Abbey Bank Noddle but other than this the climbing is more gradual.
START: Large layby on the western side of Byland Abbey, a short distance outside the hamlet. GR SE 546 785.
TIME: 3¼ to 3¾ hours not including any visit that you might make to Byland Abbey.
ACCESS: The route is all on public rights of way.
DOGS: As the route is all on public rights of way then dogs are allowed. However, as you'll see, there are frequent signs to keep them under close control, i.e. on a lead.

GRID REFERENCES

Layby	546 785
Path/lane junction	553 794
Track junction	550 796
Stile	547 798
Track junction	545 799
Path/track junction	541 802
Stile and gate	541 805
Mount Snever Observatory	537 805
Cam House	542 814
Track junction	538 816

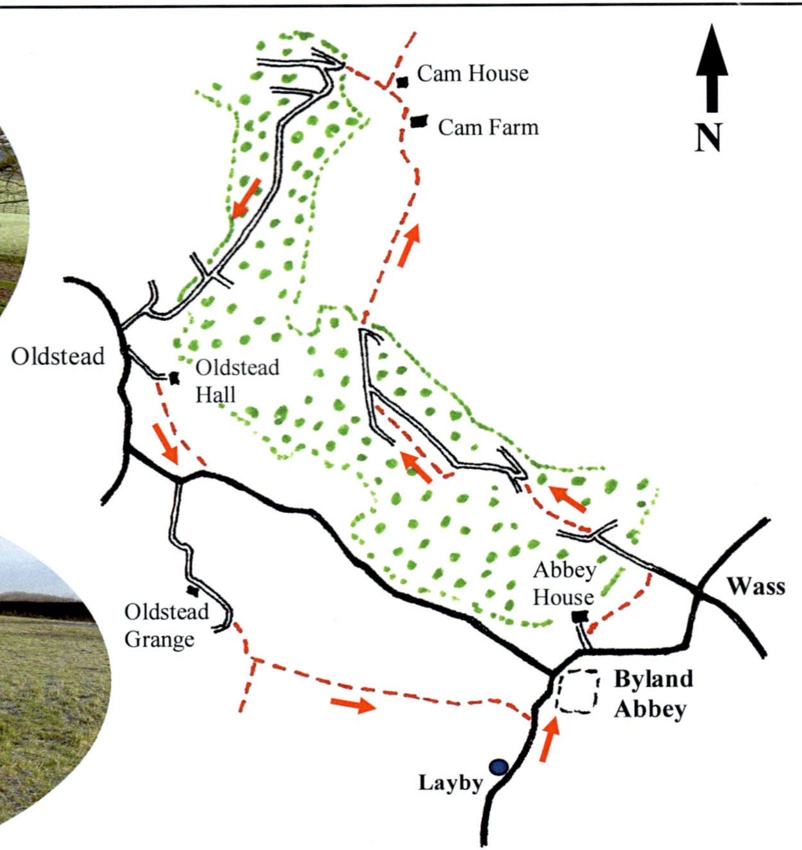

The track leading to Abbey House.

The road heading away from the layby towards Byland Abbey.

Track junction	534 807
Lane/road junction	530 805
Gate and signpost	532 801
Path/road junction	534 798
Stream crossing	535 792
Gate	545 789
Layby	546 785

FGS GRADING

Grading is T6 [D1, N1, T1, R1, H2]

Distance	**1**	6 – 12 miles
Navigation	**1**	Basic navigation skills needed
Terrain	**1**	50 – 75% on graded track or path, 25 – 50% off track
Remoteness	**1**	Countryside in fairly close proximity to habitation – at least 80% of the route within 2 miles
Height	**2**	Over 125 ft per mile

THE WALK

1. From the layby, head eastwards following the road up the rise and down the other side into the hamlet of Byland Abbey. Here an interesting diversion can be made into the Abbey itself for a visit.

Continue along the road and a couple of hundred metres after passing the abbey come to a footpath sign on the right side of the road that points up the access drive for Abbey House which lies on the left-side of the road. Here turn left to leave the road and go down the drive and after 10/15 metres come to a way-marked stile on the right-side of the drive.

Turn right to cross the stile and go across the small field to the visible stile opposite. Cross this second stile and now, following the direction of the waymarker on the stile, bear diagonally left, going up the slope of the field to come to a small gate in the upper field corner.

Go through and, again following the waymarker, bear left to a gate and once through that, continue straight ahead to another gate that leads out onto a tarmac lane at the top end of the village of Wass. **GR 553 794.**

2. Turn left to follow the lane and after a couple of metres it becomes a track leading to Lund Farm. Continue along the track as it slowly climbs until you eventually come to a T-junction with a waymarked pedestrian gate straight ahead, next to a signpost marked Cam Farm and Observatory. **GR 550 796.**

3. Go through the gate and follow the well-walked path straight ahead as it follows the left-hand fence. After a couple of hundred metres, the path bends to the right and leaves the fence, climbing slightly and passing a couple of marker posts. The path then passes through a patch of trees before coming to a waymarked stile leading into the woods. **GR 547 798.**

The track downhill from the signpost to Cam Farm.

4. Cross the stile onto the track on the other side and turn left, following the signpost to Cam Farm, to head downhill. At the bottom of the slope, cross a small stream and then start climbing up the other side and within a couple of metres come to a junction of tracks. Bear right to continue uphill and after a little distance come to a second junction. **GR 545 799.**

5. Here leave the track, which goes both left and right, and follow the footpath waymarkers as the path goes straight ahead up the bank and through the trees. Partway up the slope, the path bears right to continue climbing up to the top of the ridge of Abbey Bank Noddle.

Continue following the path as it runs along the narrow ridge. Unfortunately the vegetation prevents most of the views that you would normally associate with a ridge walk. Eventually the path joins a vehicle track. **GR 541 802.**

6. Turn right to follow the track, going past a junction on the right, and continue straight ahead to come to a waymarked stile and gate leading into open fields. **GR 541 805.**

7. At this point you do have an option of an out and back diversion of 400 metres to visit the Mount Snever Observatory. Strictly speaking this is not a public right of way although you do follow a National Park waymarked path and access is allowed.

Don't go straight through the gate, instead turn left to follow the rough track next to the right-hand wall. After a short distance you'll start to pass a series of deep ditches on the left that are known as the Camp Holes.

Looking very much like the remains of some prehistoric earthwork, Camp Holes is actually a series of irregular ditches and quarries, some up to 4 metres (14 feet) deep. They are thought to be the remains of a Medieval stone quarry.

The track now comes to a junction. Here follow the waymarkers to bear left and follow the path deeper into the woods. After a couple of hundred metres the path comes to the side of the old observatory. **GR 537 805.**

Built during 1837/38, the tower stands in the middle of the woods that cover the top of Mount Snever. It was erected by a local builder, J. Dodds, for John Wormald of Oldstead Hall to celebrate the coming of Queen Victoria to the throne. The tower housed a telescope and was used as an observatory with the owner making regular trips up a steep path at the front of the hill. One curious aspect of the building is the poem carved into a stone plaque at the front of the tower. Its an adaption of the poem 'Windsor Forest' by Alexander Pope but with deliberate changes. Why the owner would feel the need to paraphrase the poem is unknown.

Mount Snever observatory and, inset, the plaque at the front of the tower.

8. Once you have visited the observatory, return back to the gate and stile that lead into the open fields by retracing your steps.

9. Once over the stile, follow the path next to the left-hand wall across two fields.

At the beginning of the second field, a large grassy mound on the right is the remains of a prehistoric burial mound.

The prehistoric burial mound.

When you come to the end of the second field, cross the stile and, following the waymarker, immediately turn left to follow the fence keeping it on your left. As you approach Cam Farm head for a visible waymarked gate on the left of the buildings.

Heading towards Cam Farm.

Go through and continue past the buildings and then bear slightly right of straight ahead to a visible waymarked gate in front of Cam House. Once through the gate, go straight ahead to the marker post on the corner of the garden wall. **GR 542 814.**

10. Continue ahead to the next marker post and here ignore the path marked as going right and go straight ahead to the waymarked gate in front that leads onto a track. When you are through the gate, ignore the right-hand track and continue on the track straight ahead, going downhill into the valley and Great Cockerdale Wood. After a while you'll come to a track junction with a footpath marker post on the right-hand side. **GR 538 816.**

Heading down into Great Cockerdale Wood.

11. Turn left following the direction for Oldstead and follow the track as you continue to head downhill. As you descend, you'll come to a junction with a track on the right but stay with the main track as it bears left to go past a marker post and a large green container and cross to the other side of the valley. Stay on this main track as it slowly heads downhill, ignoring several footpath marker posts that point off to the right, until you eventually come to a junction with a track on the left, just in front of a wooden gate. **GR 534 807.**

12. Here continue straight ahead, round the gate and past the old Sunblest wagon, to come to a junction with a tarmac lane. Continue straight ahead to follow the lane as it heads away from the woods. Stay with the lane as it first bends right, then later sharply left before finally arriving at the side of a road next to a house. **GR 530 805.**

13. Turn left and follow the road for about 50 metres, till you come to the entrance of the drive for Oldstead Hall, which lies on the left-side of the road with a footpath marker post on the right-side. Here leave the road to turn left and follow the drive.

Just in front of the buildings, you'll come to some footpath markers on the right-side of the track. Here leave the track to follow the markers up the bank and over the stile. Once across, turn left to follow the fence and then when you come to the fence in front, turn right for a short but steep climb up the bank to a way-marked pedestrian gate at the top.

Go through the gate and follow the path between the fences to come to another small gate and a footpath signpost. **GR 532 801.**

14. Ignore the path on the right and continue straight ahead, with the hedge on your left, across two fields to come to a stile and gate. Cross the stile and follow the path between the fences as it slowly descends to come to the side of a road. **GR 534 798.**

15. Turn right to follow the road for a short distance until you come to a foot-path marker post on the right-side pointing down the drive to Oldstead Grange and Wakendale House on the left-side of the road. Here turn left to head down the drive.

As you approach the first building, a waymarker nailed to a tree directs you off the drive and down a track towards a barn. When you get to the barn, follow the markers that direct you right to pass the front of it and then left to go down the side, between the buildings and through a gateway onto a green track.

Ignore the branch of the track that goes right and continue straight ahead. The track now descends and at the bottom of the bank passes a waymarker on a tree before crossing a stream. **GR 535 792.**

16. Immediately after crossing the stream, you'll come to a second waymarker, this one on a post, that directs you left onto a path through the trees. Follow the path as it goes through a section of woodland before entering a field where you'll find a signpost for Byland Abbey.

Following the signpost, continue straight ahead down the left-side of the field. When you come to the field corner, turn left to continue along the field edge and arrive at another signpost. Here ignore the right-hand path and continue straight ahead over the stile, still making for Byland Abbey, and follow the left-hand hedge.

When you arrive at the bottom of the field, you'll come to a stile and gate on the left. Cross the stile and immediately turn right, passing another Byland Abbey signpost, to come to another stile in the field corner.

Cross this stile and continue to follow the hedge but now with it on your right and with a stream alongside it. At the end of this field, cross the stile into the second field and then when you cross the stile into the third field, leave the right -hand fence to head for the visible waymarked gate next to the tree opposite. **GR 545 789.**

17. When you have gone through the gate into the next field, you encounter a series of undulations in the surface of the ground.

As you go through the gate you are faced with the field in front which, with no better definition, is a mass of dips, hollows, and mounds. This field and the others surrounding it were part of the Byland Abbey complex and in particular this field containing the abbey's fishponds and associated dams, drains, and water channels. During the Middle Ages fish were an important part of the diet especially in religious houses where the rule on eating fish on Friday and abstaining from meat was strictly observed. As a result many of the abbeys and monasteries of the time had developed fish farming to a very high standard.

The hollows and mounds of the old fishponds.

Follow the path diagonally across the field to the left-hand fence where there is a signpost half-way up the field. Once there, follow the left-hand edge to come to a stile that leads onto the roadside. Turn right to follow the road the short distance back to the layby and the car.

Deep in the heart of Boltby Forest.
Walk 3: Boltby Forest.

WALK 3: BOLTBY FOREST

The western escarpment of the Hambleton Hills is often steep, in particular around Sutton Bank where it is often cliff-like. This means that the agricultural use that this land can be put to is often limited and as a result a number of forests and woods have been developed over the years. Boltby Forest is one of these

This walk explores the forest, often using rarely-trod paths to go deep within the woods. As an antidote to moorland and hilltop walking this could not be bettered.

The walk starts from Sneck Yate, the name derives from the local pronunciation of the word gate - 'yate', coupled with the fact that the gate had a sneck or latch, in essence the gate with the latch. The gate probably spanned the old Hambleton Drove Road which is followed at the start of the walk.

DISTANCE: 7.6 miles / 12.2 km.
ASCENT: 738 feet / 225 metres.
TERRAIN: Mainly forest path and track. After wet weather some of the paths can be quite muddy. As the forest is sited along the side of the Hambleton Hills then it is not a flat walk but rather more accurately described as undulating with a number of climbs and descents although nothing that could be described as serious.
START: Sneck Yate car park, GR SE 510 877.
TIME: 3¾ to 4¼ hours.
ACCESS: Boltby Forest is Forestry Commission owned and therefore the public has open access to the land except in cases where there is active forestry operations in progress. In these occurrences please obey all safety notices that you encounter. The route to and from the forest itself is on public rights of way.
DOGS: Dogs are allowed on the land however, please keep them under close control especially if you do encounter any forestry operations.

GRID REFERENCES

Sneck Yate car park	510 877
Track junction	505 890
Boltby Forest entrance	502 895
Gate	495 902
Marker post	486 899
Fence corner	482 898

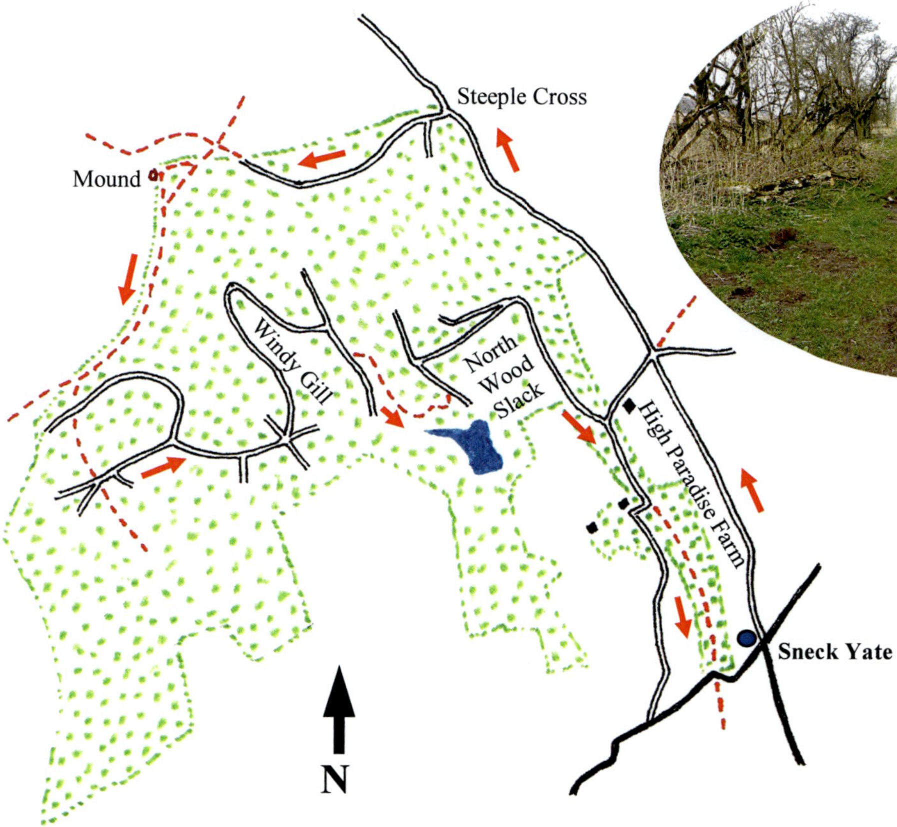

Top. The Hambleton Road leading away from the Sneck Yate car park at the start of the walk. Bottom. Going through the top of Boltby Forest.

Path junction	482 896
Path junction	478 888
Path/track junction	479 884
Track junction	486 885
Track crossroads	488 886
Track junction	489 891
Track/path junction	490 890
Path/track junction	496 888
Track junction	494 889
Track junction	498 893
Track/lane junction	503 886
Track/road junction	507 876
Sneck Yate car park	510 877

FGS GRADING

Grading is T3 [D1, N1, T0, R1, H0]

Distance	**1**	6 – 12 miles
Navigation	**1**	Basic navigation skills needed
Terrain	**0**	75% + on graded track or path
Remoteness	**1**	Countryside in fairly close proximity to habitation – at least 80% of the route within 2 miles
Height	**0**	Less than 100 ft per mile

THE WALK

1. From the Sneck Yate parking space follow the Hambleton Road, which despite it's grand name is more of a track, northwards. This former drove road follows a very wide walled lane between fields until it eventually comes to a corner where the track itself, turns left through a gate. Here there is a Cleveland Way signpost on the left, bridleway markers going through a gate on the right and an information board. **GR 505 890.**

2. Continue on the track going straight ahead and after a little while you'll come to a gate leading into Boltby Forest. **GR 502 895.**

3. Go through the open gap next to the gate and, ignoring the track on the left, follow the right-hand gravel path as it runs along just on the inside of the forest. After a while the path comes to a gate that leads out of the forest onto the open moor. **GR 495 902.**

Before you continue on the route it is worth popping through the gate to view two ancient monuments that lie just on the other side.

The remains of Steeple Cross lie on the right side of the track, just on the other side of the gate. Built during the Medieval period, which means that the cross could be anything up to 1,000 years old, the cross acted as a waymarker for travellers on the forerunner of the Drove Road. It is one of many that were erected across the moors in response to an instruction by the magistrates of Northallerton who were concerned about travellers finding their way across these hills.

It is difficult to judge the size of the original cross. Over the years it has become significantly eroded and now only part of the weathered shaft and the base remain, the remaining section of shaft only standing 0.7 metres (2 ft) above the ground. The cross is a scheduled ancient monument.

Alongside the cross lies the western end of the Steeple Cross Dyke. The dyke is visible as an earthwork ditch with two flanking banks, one either side. This earthwork is a Cross Ridge Dyke and runs for approximately 2 km across the width of the Hambleton Hills. It is thought that the dyke originally ran from Windy Gill in the west to Stony Gill in the east. Unfortunately, from this point the western section to Windy Gill has been destroyed by the planting of Boltby Forest.

Dating back to the late Bronze Age or early Iron Age, making it possibly 3,000 years old, the dyke forms part of the Cleave Dyke system. This is a series of dykes and ditches that formed either territorial or field boundaries across much of the Hambleton Hills. Another part of this system of earthworks was visited on Walk 1.

The remains of Steeple Cross Dyke and, inset, Steeple Cross.

4. Don't go through the gate but instead turn left to follow the track on that side, round the gate and down into the trees. After a 100 metres you'll come to a crossroads and here, go straight ahead passing a bridleway marker post.

Continue on this track as it initially climbs slightly but then begins a descent. Eventually you'll come to a marker post. **GR 486 899.**

Here the track, which is more of a path now, enters an open area with no tree cover and starts to bend to the left a short distance in front of a visible way-marked gate. Stay on the path as it curves round and within a short distance you'll come to a path crossroads next to a fence corner.

Ignore the bridleway marker that directs you straight ahead and instead turn right to follow the path along the edge of the trees. After around 200 metres you'll come to both the forest and the fence corner. **GR 482 898.**

As you get to the corner of the fence, a large heather-covered earth mound confronts you on the other side of the fence. The mound stands 10 metres (30 ft) in diameter and over 1 metre (4 ft) high and can be seen from a fair distance. Built during the Bronze Age, 2,600 to 700 BC, the mound may be up to 4,000 years old.

It is a round barrow, built to house the remains of the dead and it is one of eight of these large structures that line the top western edge of Kepwick and Boltby Moors. At some point in the past this one has been excavated as there is a large hole in its centre although there is no record of what was discovered.

5. Don't leave the forest but instead turn left to follow the path along the edge of the trees. The path here follows the side of Windygill Ridge and gives some superb views over the lower hills at the side of the Hambletons and the Vale of Mowbray. After a little while the path comes to a junction with a second path. **GR 482 896.**

6. Here ignore the bridleway marker post to your left and turn right to follow the path along the top of the ridge. Being at the edge of the forest you have an open aspect to the right but at the time of writing, the Forestry Commission had also harvested the trees to the left giving an open view to both sides.

Eventually the path passes a gate on the right that leads onto the open moor and a couple of hundred metres after that comes to a footpath marker post and a junction with a path on the left. **GR 478 888.**

7. Here leave the main path to turn left and descend down the side-path over the edge and down the side of the ridge. After a couple of hundred metres the path goes straight over a rough track and continues to descend.

After a little while the path starts to level out a bit and makes its way through an area of felled trees. The path is fairly obvious to follow but here it can be a bit wet and boggy especially after wet weather. The path does eventually meet up with a track at a three-way junction. **GR 479 884.**

8. Here, ignore the path which continues straight on over the track, and instead turn left. Follow the track as it begins a gradual climb and passes two rough tracks in quick succession, one on the right and one on the left.

Eventually the track bends to the right before starting to head downhill and passing another rough track on the right (**GR 486 885**) to finally come to a cross roads. **GR 488 886.**

9. Take the second turning on the left, which is the obvious well-made track on the left, and follow it as it goes up the side of Windy Gill. Not that you'll spot the gill, it lies hidden among the trees below you. The track starts a long right-hand bend to curve round the top and finally cross, the gill itself and then descends to come to a track junction. **GR 489 891.**

10. Turn right here to head downhill and after 100/150 metres come to a path on the left side of the track, just before the track crosses a stream gully. There are no waymarkers at the junction of the track and path. **GR 490 890.**

The path leading off the side of the track.

11. Turn left to leave the track and follow the path which shadows the left side of the stream. The path follows the route of an old track which is little used now except as a path and cuts deep into the heart of the forest. One of the most delightful stretches of this walk as the path weaves in and out of the trees.

After a while the path crosses a side-stream, which flows into the main stream that you have been following, and here joins another path. Turn right here to continue down through the trees.

Crossing the side-stream.

The path continues for about 300 metres to come to a faint junction that can be easily missed where a minor path leaves the right side of the main path and goes off into the trees. Here stay left and follow the main path as it begins to bend to the left and then climbs for a short distance to reach the side of a vehicle track. **GR 496 888.**

12. Turn left here to follow the track uphill and after a few hundred metres come to a junction. **GR 494 889.**

13. Turn right and continue to climb for a little while before the track levels out. After 400 metres the track comes to another junction. **GR 498 893.**

14. Here turn right to follow the track as it curves round the head of Northwoods Slack. After a while the track begins a steady climb and when you get to the top of the bank, go round the gate and come to a crossroads. Turn right here and you'll quickly come to a second junction where the track joins the side of a tarmac lane and also meets the Cleveland Way although there are no Cleveland Way markers at this point to tell you. **GR 503 886.**

15. Turn right here to follow the tarmac lane for 300/400 metres until you come to the point where it turns sharply right to head downhill. Here leave the lane to continue straight ahead, following the Cleveland Way markers, going through a gate and heading across a field.

At the end of the field, go through a second gate and follow a broad track as it climbs up through the woods. Eventually the track comes to the side of a road. **GR 507 876.**

16. Turn left to follow the road uphill for 250 metres to come back to Sneck Yate car park and the opportunity to rest your feet.

Heading towards the woods after Murton Grange and, inset, the ponds of Nettle Dale.
Walk 4: The Eastern Dales.

WALK 4: THE EASTERN DALES

The eastern side of the Hambleton Hills are cut by a large number of narrow, wooded dales many of which feed into the valley of the River Rye, which borders the Hambleton's on this side. This walk explores a couple of these small dales and their woods and along the way comes across a surprising reminder of the monks from Rievaulx Abbey.

DISTANCE: 8.4 miles / 13.5 km.
ASCENT: 1,312 feet / 400 metres.
TERRAIN: Mainly field and woodland paths and tracks. There is a bit of climbing on this walk mainly caused by going down into the valleys and then coming back out again. Some of these climbs may be quite steep.
START: The centre of the village of Cold Kirby. GR SE 533 845. There is ample roadside parking on the approaches into and around the village green. Park considerately and don't inconvenience local residents.
TIME: 4¼ to 4¾ hours.
ACCESS: This route is all on public rights of way.
DOGS: As the route is all on rights of way then dogs are allowed but please keep them under close control. You will encounter livestock in some of the fields including cattle, which during the spring may have young calves with them.

GRID REFERENCES

Cold Kirby village green	533 845
Track/road junction	531 852
Track/road junction	531 861
Wood entrance	532 866
Bridge	531 869
Track/road junction	536 875
Road/track junction	536 879
Track junction	546 877
Gate	553 875
Track junction	559 875
Barnclose Farm	566 871
Lane/road junction	566 855
Reirs Farm	560 854
Gate	556 852
Track crossroads	556 847

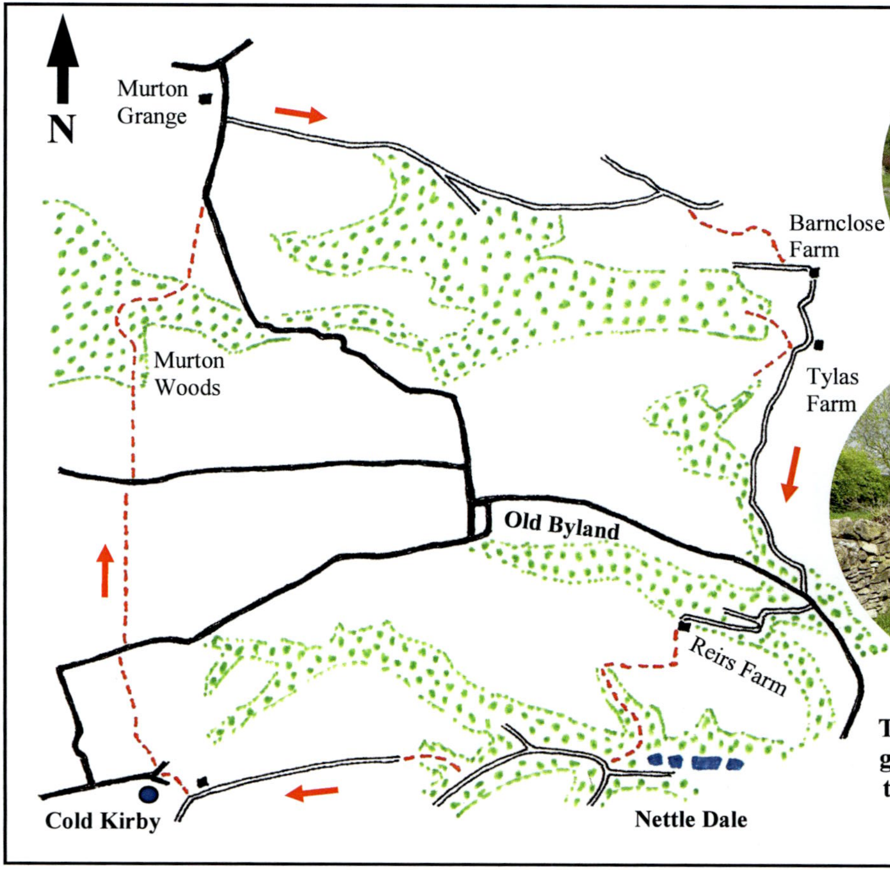

Top, going past Cold Kirby village green at the start of the walk. Bottom, the path through the narrow field as you exit the village.

Track crossroads	552 847
Track/path junction	549 846
Cold Kirby	533 845

FGS GRADING
Grading is T5 [D1, N1, T0, R1, H2]

Distance	**1**	6 – 12 miles
Navigation	**1**	Basic navigation skills needed
Terrain	**0**	75% + on graded track or path
Remoteness	**1**	Countryside in fairly close proximity to habitation – at least 80% of the route within 2 miles
Height	**2**	Over 125 ft per mile

THE WALK

1. Follow the road into the village and when it bears right to go to the church, continue straight ahead. About 100 metres after this junction you'll come to a bridleway signpost that points up a drive on the left that goes to Ailred Barn.

Turn left to follow the drive into the yard behind the building and then go through the white gate, swiftly followed by a smaller gate and into a narrow field. At the end of this field, go through another gate and then follow a grass track down to a signpost. Once here, bear right to follow the track up to yet another gate.

Go through and once in the next field, follow the left-hand fence over a small hill. Descend down the other side to a gate that leads onto the side of a road. **GR 531 852.**

2. Turn right to go along the road for a few metres to a bridleway signpost and a gate on the left-side of the road. Go through the small gate to the right of the main one and follow the path alongside the left-hand wall. After a little while the path becomes more of a track, still running alongside the wall. This track

The flat tops of the Hambleton Hills can often spring a few surprises not least the fact that a number of them are cultivated with cereal crops and also used for livestock. However, during the middle ages the view across this landscape would have been very much different with a wide open view of grass pastures filled with large flocks of sheep grazing across the hill tops. These hills provided the grazing for the great abbeys of Rievaulx and Byland and upon whose flocks, the great wealth and power of these two abbeys was built.

Passing through the fields on the top of the Hambleton Hills and, inset, cattle grazing on the outskirts of Cold Kirby.

goes over another small hill, descends into a dip then starts climbing again to come to a gate that leads onto a road. **GR 531 861.**

3. Again, turn right along the road for a few metres to come to a bridleway marker post and a gate on the left-hand side. Go through the gate and follow the fence on the right. When you get to the fence corner, bear right to stay with the fence and go round the edge of the field and come to a gate leading into a wood. **GR 532 866**.

4. Go through the gate, or more accurately around it, onto a path which bears to the left to descend down into the woods. After you've descended for a little while, you'll pass a signpost to 'Murton' and shortly after that the path forks but

Entering Murton Woods.

does re-join again after it has passed a boggy bit. Eventually you'll come to the valley floor where the path crosses a stream via a narrow bridge. **GR 531 869.**

5. Cross the bridge, go through the gate and then cross the footbridge. When you are on the other side, follow the rough track in front that goes steeply uphill to arrive at a waymarked gate.

Pass through the gate onto a track, next to a signpost, and here turn right to follow the track uphill. After a little while you'll pass a staggered crossroads of tracks but here just continue straight ahead, still climbing. As you do finally approach the top of the bank, you'll pass a bridleway signpost on the right but ignore this to continue straight ahead.

Once at the top of the bank, the track bears left to go through a gap to enter a field where it follows the right-hand wall and makes for the distant buildings of Murton Grange. At the end of the field, pass through a gate to come to the side of a road as it goes round a bend. **GR 536 875.**

6. Continue straight ahead along the road, still making for the white buildings of Murton Grange. However, just before you come to them, you'll come to a track on the right-side of the road with a bridleway marker post pointing up it. **GR 536 879.**

7. Turn right here to leave the road and follow the track across the fields, heading towards a distant wood. When you get to the woods, the track bends to the left to run along the left-hand edge of the wood.

After a while you'll come to a junction where the main track bends to the right to go deeper into the woods and a more minor track continues straight ahead along the wood's edge. **GR 546 877.**

8. Leave the main track to continue straight ahead on the minor track. Eventually at the end of the woods you'll come to a waymarked gate. **GR 553 875.**

9. Go through the gate and continue straight ahead keeping to the left of the fence. At the end of the field, pass through the gate and go straight ahead on the track to pass to the left of the building and come to a track junction with a marker post over on the right. **GR 559 875.**

Leaving the track to follow the marker post towards the rise and, inset, the marker post on top of the rise.

10. Don't follow the track here, instead bear right to follow the direction of the right-hand waymarker and head for a visible second marker post on the top of the rise in front. When you get to this marker post, follow the path along the ridge and after a little while it descends down to a waymarked gate slightly to your left.

Go through and immediately turn left to follow the edge of the field as it descends. When you get to the bottom of the field, ignore the stile across the fence and, following the blue bridleway marker, turn right to head alongside a line of trees, keeping them on your right.

At the end of the trees, you'll come to a marker post and here turn left onto a track and descend to Barnclose Farm, passing through a gate before entering the yard. **GR 566 871.**

11. In the yard, turn right at the marker post and follow the access drive away from the farm. Stay on this main tarmac lane, ignoring the side turning to Tylas Cottage, and climb up to Tylas Farm.

The area around Tylas Farm was the original site of Byland Abbey, visited on Walk 2 Byland Abbey and Mount Snever, before it was moved to its current location near Ampleforth. Fleeing from Scottish raids across the border, the monks left Calder in Cumbria during the 1130's and after a year of wandering were given land near Tylas Farm on which to build a new monastery. However, the close proximity of the already well-established Rievaulx Abbey caused a little bit of distress to the brothers of both abbeys as the bells of each could be clearly heard at both locations. Being the later arrivals in the valley, the monks of Byland gave way and in 1147 moved to Oldstead and then later Byland where the soaring structure that is Byland Abbey was built.

The lane now turns right before turning left again and here ignore first the foot-path marker and second the bridleway marker, both on the right of the lane, and continue to follow the lane itself.

Stay with the lane as it follows an undulating course along the valley floor. Eventually it starts to rise up the side of the valley and here views of the distant Rievaulx Abbey can be seen straight ahead. As it climbs, the lane now enters the wood above and passes a track going downhill on the left, before arriving at the side of a road. **GR 566 855.**

12. Turn left to follow the road for about 100 metres to reach a track on the right-side of the road that has a bridleway marker pointing down it. Turn right here to leave the road and, ignoring the second bridleway marker on the left, follow the track as it descends down to the valley floor.

When you get there, cross the stream and ignoring the track on the right, continue to follow the obvious main track as it starts the long slog of the climb up the other side of the valley. When you do finally get to the top of the bank, the track bears left into Reirs Farm. **GR 560 854.**

13. Following the marker post, turn right and when you get to the end of the buildings, turn left between two barns to go to the waymarked gate in front. Pass through the gate to enter the field and then head across it making for another gate at the bottom right-side of the field, next to the trees.

Go through and immediately turn right to follow the fence, keeping it on your right, to come to another gate. Again, go through and continue straight ahead, following the field edge to come to yet another gate. **GR 556 852.**

14. Go through the gate and immediately turn left to follow the path that descends down the small wooded valley. As the path nears the bottom of the descent, it bears to the right and the valley opens out.

Continue descending to come to the edge of one of the four ponds of Nettle Dale and here turn right to come to a gate. Pass through and follow what is now a track as it comes to a ford and footbridge. Cross the bridge to come to a staggered track crossroads. **GR 556 847.**

The pond in front is one of the four large fish ponds in Nettle Dale that were built during the 12th century by the monks of nearby Rievaulx Abbey. During the Middle Ages fish, especially fresh water fish, was seen as a valuable food source and formed a much larger part of the diet than it does nowadays. Whereas we think of fish farms as being a relatively modern invention, the monks of the various medieval abbeys had developed and established the science of fisheries to a surprisingly high level.

The fish ponds of Nettle Dale.

15. Turn right to follow the Cleveland Way, which is now followed back to Cold Kirby, as it goes along the track. After a little while you'll come to a track crossroads. **GR 552 847.**

16. Turn left here, following the Cleveland Way signpost, to follow the track as it goes up the side-valley of Flassen Dale. After approximately 300metres you'll come to another junction and Cleveland Way signpost on the right-side of the track. **GR 549 846.**

Heading up Flassen Dale.

17. Leave the main track to turn right here and continue to follow the Cleveland Way as it makes it's way on a path up the little side-valley. As you approach the top of the bank go through a gate and stile and continue climbing to the bank top where you emerge into a field. Here follow the left-hand fence across the field to come to a waymarked gate and stile.

Once across, follow the track on the other side as it goes straight ahead. The track is followed for quite a while until you pass a farm on the right-hand side of it. Just after the farm, the track bends to the left and here on the right-side of the track, a Cleveland Way signpost points you down a path. Leave the track to follow the path as it goes down a bank before curving round and then climbing back up to enter Cold Kirby not far from the village green and your car.

Climbing up Hood Hill and, inset, going along the ridge of the hill. Walk 5: Hood Hill.

WALK 5: HOOD HILL

Hood Hill stands as an isolated hill separated from the main Hambleton Hills escarpment and is surrounded by the Forestry Commission woodland of Kilburn Woods, whose trees stretch up almost to the summit ridge itself. This is a hill that has a chequered past, both in folklore and history with links to ancient druids, the devil, a long-lost Norman castle and the mysterious crash of a state-of-the-art RAF fighter.

DISTANCE: 5.4 miles / 8.7 km.
ASCENT: 1,040 feet / 317 metres.
TERRAIN: The route is all on woodland paths and tracks. Considering that this is only a relatively small area of woodland, the route is very undulating with some steep climbs especially the long drag up Hood Hill itself.
START: The White Horse and Kilburn Woods car park situated just underneath the White Horse. GR SE 514 812.
TIME: 3 to 3½ hours.
ACCESS: Although not on public rights of way, the walk is all within Kilburn Woods, a Forestry Commission owned woodland and this means that the public has right of access throughout the entire woodland.
DOGS: Dogs are allowed although it may be advisable to keep them on a lead as you go over the top of Hood Hill as there are a couple of steep drops to either side.

GRID REFERENCES

White Horse car park	514 812
Path junction	513 818
Path/track junction	516 824
Track junction	507 816
Track/path junction	507 818
Path junction	506 818
Path junction	505 816
Path crossroads	504 816
Hood Hill	504 814
Path junction	504 811
Marker posts	501 808
Path junction	500 807
Path/track junction	501 815
Track junction	504 816

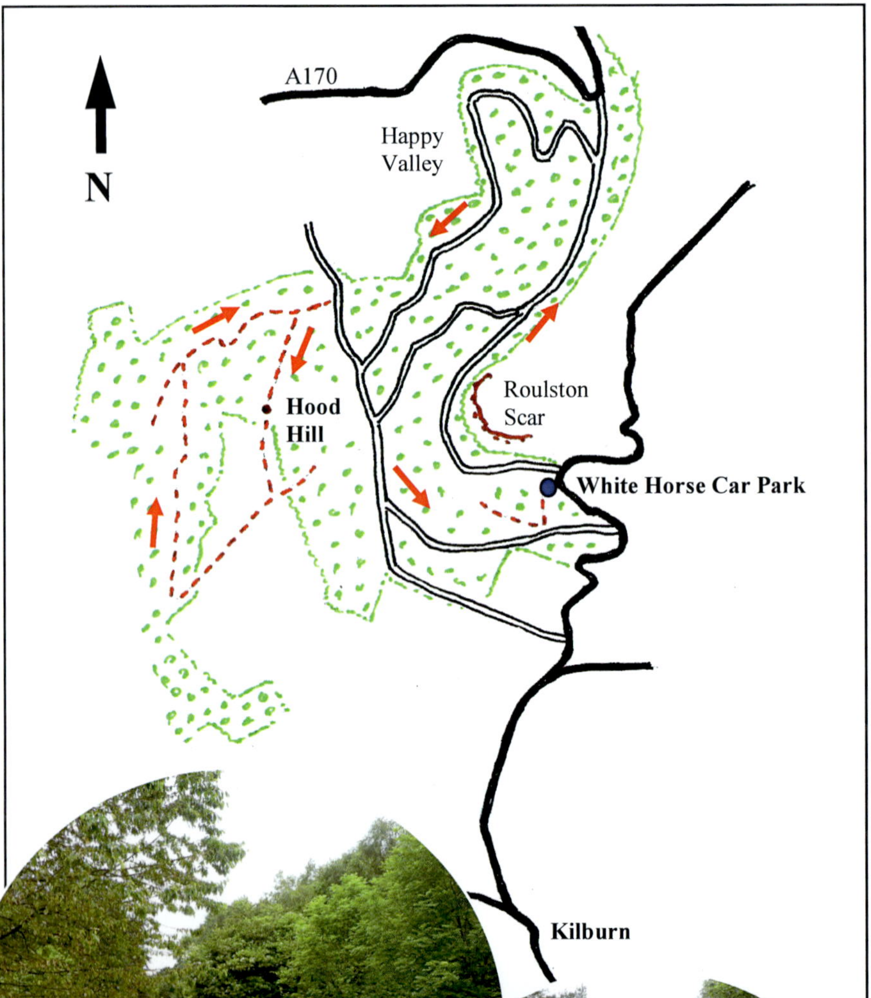

The start of the walk, going round the gate from the car park and following the path as it heads away.

Track/path junction	506 818
Track junction	507 818
Track junction	507 816
Track/path crossroads	508 814
Track/path junction	508 812
Track/path junction	514 810
Car park	514 812

FGS GRADING

Grading is T5 [D0, N1, T1, R1, H2]

Distance	**0**	Up to 6 miles
Navigation	**1**	Basic navigation skills needed
Terrain	**1**	50 – 75% on graded track or path, 25 – 50% off track
Remoteness	**1**	Countryside in fairly close proximity to habitation – at least 80% of the route within 2 miles
Height	**2**	Over 125 ft per mile

THE WALK

1. From the top end of the car park, go round the gate onto the forest path and follow it. After a short distance you'll come to a path junction and here, ignore the green marker pointing left, take the right-hand branch and follow it as it starts to go uphill.

The path undulates a bit, going up and then downhill again, before passing underneath the cliffs of Roulston Scar over on the right. Eventually you'll come to a junction of paths. **GR 513 818.**

The prominent cliffs of Roulston Scar form the western escarpment of the North York Moors, rising up from the Vale of Mowbray to a height of 280 metres (919 feet), they are the third highest point on the Hambleton Hills.

The prominent cliffs of Roulston Scar.

2. Here, ignore the right-hand branch that goes steeply uphill and continue straight ahead to come, after a few metres, to a bridleway signpost. Again, continue straight ahead, ignoring the bridleway which goes off down to the left. Eventually the path comes to the side of a track. **GR 516 824.**

3. Turn left here and follow the track as it heads downhill. The track twists and turns as it heads downhill before it eventually takes a long, sweeping bend to the left to pass through the top of Happy Valley where the fields can be seen through the trees on the right. The track now starts to climb again before eventually coming to a track junction. **GR 507 816.**

In his 1906 book, 'Richmondshire and the Vale of Mowbray', Edmund Bogg recounts the local legend about Happy Valley. In the distant past, this spot was a secluded and sacred retreat of the old druids. As Christianity started to make inroads into the country the local chieftain had the problem of which faith he and his people should follow, the old religion or the new one from the east. To help decide, he announced a great assembly in the Valley and invited both druids and Christian priests to address it. The decision on which faith to follow being decided by the most persuasive.

Happy Valley seen through the trees.

4. Turn right at the junction to follow the track as it starts to slowly go uphill. After 200 metres and just as the track starts to level out, come to a path junction on the left that is marked by a couple of posts. **GR 507 818.**

The junction marked by the couple of posts.

5. Leave the track here to turn left and follow the main path, not the left-hand mountain bike path, up the hill. There now follows a steady climb up through the trees to come to a junction with a marker post. **GR 506 818.**

Following the path up through the trees.

6. Ignore the marker which directs you right and continue straight ahead up the front of the hill. After a couple of hundred metres you'll come to another path junction (**GR 505 816**) and here take the right-hand path to continue the steady climb uphill.

You'll have only been climbing for another 50 metres or so before you now come to a path crossroads (**GR 504 816**). Continue straight ahead, still going uphill. However, it's not long now before you get to the top of the hill. **GR 504 814.**

7. Continue on the path as it now goes down into a dip and up the other side before then following the line of the ridge.

As the assembly gathered in Happy Valley to decide which religion to follow, the devil decided to make mischief and steer the gathering away from the ways of Christianity. Disguising himself as a druid, the devil entered the debate certain that his words would sway the audience. However, one of the Christian priests was so eloquent that there was little doubt as to which faith would be chosen. Enraged that his words had been bettered, the devil hurled his disguise aside and cursing the people below leapt to the top of Roulston Scar. Here the priests attempted to cast him out and in his eagerness to flee, he caught a large boulder with his foot and this stone landed with a thump on the summit of Hood Hill.

Weighing around 20 ton, the stone still bore the mark of the devil's foot and, according to local legend, was later used by the druids for sacrifice. Called "The Altar" by locals, the stone became a local landmark and can be seen on old photographs of the area. It was this stone that was hit by Flying Officer Grabham's Sabre when it plummeted to the ground. The impact shattering the stone and creating the dip that you walk down into and then back out of.

Going down into the heavily overgrown dip and, inset, the steps going out of the dip.

Shown on the OS map as earthworks, the summit of Hood Hill is thought to be the location of Hood Castle. The earthworks that surround the summit of the hill form a small enclosure with the castle being built under the motte and bailey design, a large wooden or stone-built keep erected on a raised bank of earth, or in this case the hill itself, surrounded by an outer wall or palisade. The castle may have been constructed by Robert de Stuteville at some point between 1086 and 1106. It is known that a licence to crenellate the castle was granted in 1264, these fortifications including a provision for a dyke and a wall of stone. The last mention of the castle was in 1322 and from then it appears to have disappeared from history.

With steep descents on both sides, the ridge gives good views out over the Vale of Mowbray and over towards Kilburn. After a while, the path starts to descend down the front of the ridge and comes to a path junction. **GR 504 811.**

The ridge of Hood Hill and, inset, a glider tow above the hill.

The Yorkshire Gliding Club has been sited at Sutton Bank since the 1930's. As you are following this route, and if the weather is suitable for flying, you may see a number of gliders and their towing planes in the air.

8. Here, turn right to continue the descent down the hill. After a steady descent the path comes to two marker posts (**GR 501 808**) and here, turns left to re-enter the woods and continue downhill to finally come to a path junction, again with two marker posts. **GR 500 807.**

9. Turn right to follow the path as it starts to climb slightly and then follows an undulating route round the side of the hill to come to a junction with a track. **GR 501 815.**

10. Turn right onto the track and follow it as it continues uphill. After a little while the track climbs a steep zig-zag and not long after passes to the left of an old quarry (**GR 503 817**) before coming to a junction with a track on the right. **GR 504 816.**

Climbing the steep zig-zag in the track.

11. Turn left and after a short distance the track starts to descend to come to a junction with a path on the right (**GR 506 818**). Turn left once again to continue going downhill to join another track. **GR 507 818.**

12. Turn right onto this new track and follow it as it starts to slowly climb. You'll pass a track junction on the left (**GR 507 816**) and here continue straight ahead up the hill.

Just before you get to the top of the rise, you'll come to a crossroads with a gravelled path on the left and a path on the right (**GR 508 814**). Continue straight ahead passing a track on the left just 20 metres after leaving the cross-roads.

Continue on over the rise and start to descend and not long after passing over the top, you'll come to a junction with a path on the right. **GR 508 812.**

13. Continue on the main track as it bears to the left, still heading downhill. After a little while the track starts to climb before eventually, after about 600 metres, coming to the top of a bank and meeting a path on the left complete with two marker posts. **GR 514 810.**

14. Here turn left to leave the track and follow the path back into the trees. After a couple of metres you'll come to a marker post and a second path on the right side.

Turn right here to follow this second path for a steep climb up through the trees to emerge into the bottom end of the White Horse car park where you started from several hours earlier.

On the night of Tuesday, September 21, 1954, Flying Officer Colin Grabham was returning to RAF Linton-on-Ouse after a high altitude night training flight in a Sabre F4 fighter aircraft. The Sabre was an American aircraft built under licence in Canada, that was used by the RAF in limited numbers during the mid -1950's before the introduction of more modern UK-built aircraft such as the Hawker Hunter. An hour after take-off, the 23-year-old pilot radioed the air base to say he was nearby and was given several vectors to steer. A few minutes later he was contacted by Linton Control Tower to say he was over the airfield and this signal, in turn, was acknowledged by the pilot. Then just over two minutes later, the aircraft plunged at a near vertical angle of descent into Hood Hill, hitting the Altar Stone. The pilot was killed instantly and such was the impact that the flames and the noise of the crash were seen and heard several miles away with parts of the plane being found almost a mile away from the site of the crash. The deep impact crater still lies on the line of the path as it goes over the summit of the hill. Mystery surrounds why the aircraft was above Hood Hill, the air crash investigators thought that it was likely that the pilot had thought that the lights at Topcliffe airfield, only a short distance from Sutton Bank, were those of Linton-on-Ouse, and why it plunged so dramatically out of the sky. Flying Officer Grabham's name is remembered on the memorial plaque dedicated to lost aircrew that is next to the path along the top of the escarpment of Roulston Scar and which is passed on Walk 1.

Following the track through the heather after leaving White Gill Head.
Walk 6: Arden Great Moor.

WALK 6: ARDEN GREAT MOOR

As the Hambleton Hills rise to the north they gradually gain in height and the fields and pastures give way to heather moorland. Here, although the sheep still graze, the shooting of grouse becomes dominant with grouse butts and shooter's tracks criss-crossing the moor.

This walk uses the right to roam to follow a series of these tracks across the moor. Along the way you'll come across some surprising reminders of how man has lived on and worked these hills over the ages.

DISTANCE: 9.5 miles / 15.2 km
ASCENT: 1,112 feet / 339 metres
TERRAIN: The route is on moorland track with the opening stretch out of Kepwick up to the moor along a tarmac lane. The climb out of Kepwick to the moor is a long steady one which in places can be a bit steep.
START: Small car park next to the chapel in the village of Kepwick. GR SE 467 909.
TIME: 4¼ to 4¾ hours.
ACCESS: The route uses a mixture of public rights of way and tracks over open access land.
DOGS: Not allowed on the open access land.

GRID REFERENCES

Kepwick car park	467 909
Track crossroads	489 915
White Gill Head	491 932
Track junction	501 934
Grouse butts	510 929
Burial mound	515 926
Track junction	511 916
Track junction	512 915
Track junction	510 915
Track junction	505 917
Burial mound	502 919
Track junction	491 923
Track crossroads	489 915
Kepwick car park	467 909

Photos, top, leaving the car park to head through the village and, bottom, the crossroads at the end of the village.

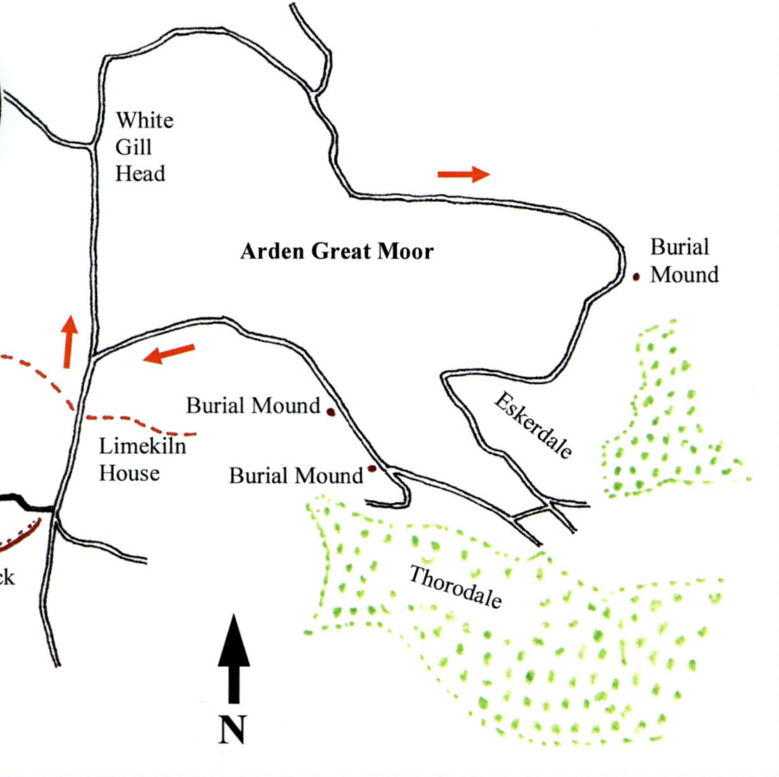

FGS Grading
Grading is F4 [D1, N1, T0, R1, H1]

Distance	**1**	6 – 12 miles
Navigation	**1**	Basic navigation skills needed
Terrain	**0**	75% + on graded track or path
Remoteness	**1**	Countryside in fairly close proximity to habitation – at least 80% of the route within 2 miles
Height	**1**	Over 100 ft per mile

THE WALK

1. Exit the car park and turn left to head through the village. At the other end, you'll come to a three-way junction where the main road turns left and the right-hand branch goes to Kepwick Hall. Here take the middle road that goes straight ahead downhill to a seasonal ford. For most of the year the ford is dry but if you do happen to come to it when it is in flood, then there is a footbridge to the left hidden amongst the vegetation.

On the other side of the ford, the road starts to climb while giving views of a distant Kepwick Hall over on the right-hand side. Stay on the road to go past, first the entrance to Stay Farm and then a little later the entrance to a lodge on the Kepwick Hall estate. Here you go past an 'unsuitable for motors' sign and the road starts to climb quite steeply and also enters an area of woodland.

Stay on the road as it zig-zags up through the woods and ignore any tracks or paths that go off on either side. After a while the road leaves the shelter of the trees and comes to a gate. At the time of test walking this was rather ramshackle, being made of a number of pallets tied together. Hopefully this will be replaced by something a bit more permanent as it is a little bit dodgy to use.

Go through the gate and continue on the road as it climbs past the extensive workings of Kepwick Quarry.

Although a quiet little village now, during the 1800's the population of Kepwick was over two hundred, all due to the workings here at Kepwick Quarry and the other smaller quarries around the front of the escarpment.

Apart from the workings themselves, the most obvious feature is the embankment that abuts either side of the road. This embankment carried an old wagonway which carried the limestone down from the quarry and three miles across the country to a set of limekilns near Leake Church which lies on the Thirsk to Stockton road.

The wagonway was opened in 1833 and crossed the road by means of a bridge. The lower section of the line was worked by horses pulling the wagons along the rails with the upper section operating by incline, the heavy, full wagons pulling the empty ones up the wagonway as they descended. The wagonway was closed in 1890.

However, it still survives as a raised embankment that can be traced throughout its full length, just stopping short of the remains of the limekilns. The wagonway is a scheduled ancient monument.

The road going through the embankment of the old wagonway and, inset, the quarry's spoil heaps.

Eventually the road comes to the top of the hill and arrives at a gate through which you pass onto a crossroads of tracks complete with Cleveland Way signpost. **GR 489 915.**

2. Turn left to follow the Cleveland Way to Osmotherley, this section of this national long distance route also being part of the old Hambleton Drove Road. Follow the track for just over 400 metres until you come to a bridleway marker post on the right-side of the track. This marks the location of Limekiln House, an old coaching house on the Drove Road.

As with most drove roads, there were regular stopping places for both the drovers and the cattle to rest, usually overnight. Known as 'stances' these stops often had an inn and land set aside for the cattle to graze. Located at this junction are the remains of Limekiln House, one of the stances located along this stretch of the drove road. It was last occupied in 1890 but still stood up to 1953 when it was demolished on safety grounds. Traces of stone walls and brickwork can still be found amongst the turf.

The stonework of the buildings and walls of Limekiln House.

Ignore the bridleway marker post and continue on the Cleveland Way for a short distance to a gate. Go through and within a few metres you'll come to a marker post and a track going off on the right. Ignore this track and continue straight ahead.

A short distance later you'll again pass another track on the right, this one going off into some disused quarries on that side. Again continue straight ahead to come to a rather strange cattle grid that doesn't seem to be connected to any fences or walls on either side.

Just past the cattle grid, you arrive at White Gill Head and here the Cleveland Way takes a sharp turn to the left and just as you turn, a second track leaves the right-hand side to head across the moor in that direction. **GR 491 932.**

3. Turn right to leave the Cleveland Way and follow this second track as it bears to the right and slowly climbs over the top of the moor to the other side of Arden Great Moor. Here the track continues to bear right to run high above the valley of the River Rye before eventually coming to a junction with a track coming up from the valley on the left. **GR 501 934.**

4. Ignore the left-hand side-track and continue on the main track as it runs along the edge of the moor high above the valley. After 900 metres the track passes between a line of grouse butts. **GR 510 929.**

Shortly after this, the track begins a long sweeping bend to the right and passes through an area of loose stones laid upon the ground. Here, a short distance away from the left-side of the track, you may spot the remains of an ancient burial mound. **GR 515 926.**

Only just visible above ground level but clearly recognisable on the left-side of the track as it looks down over the valley below, lies the remains of a round cairn. The structure has been clearly robbed out at some point in the past with just the core of the original cairn remaining.

The mound just a short distance away from the track and, inset, the mound itself.

The track now starts to descend slightly as it curves round the head of the small side-valley of Eskerdale. Once the track has gone round the valley head, it comes to a junction with a rough track on the left, **GR 511 916**.

Here continue on the main track as it now bends to the right away from the side of the valley and after about 50/60 metres you'll come to another track junction, this one next to a large hole in the ground. **GR 512 915.**

Looking down into Eskerdale.

5. Here turn right to continue across the moor and head towards the valley of Thorodale which can be seen in the near distance. After 200 metres the track bends once more to the right and comes to a junction with a faint track coming in on the left. **GR 510 915.**

Stay on the obvious main track as it continues to bear right and run high along the side of Thorodale. The track now starts to climb slightly and after 600 metres comes to a marker post and a faint track on the left that goes down into the valley. **GR 505 917.**

Here, on the left-side of the main track and a few metres to the right of the junction lie two prehistoric burial mounds.

Close to the track lie the remains of two round barrows that date back to the Bronze Age, between 2,600 and 700 BC. A round barrow is a hemispherical mound made of earth and stone in which the remains of the dead were placed. Unlike graves from the earlier Neolithic period which tended to be communal, the round barrows of the Bronze Age usually contained the remains of just the one individual. It is thought that this would be a higher ranking individual to warrant the time and effort to build these structures, such as a chieftain or priest.

Although distinctive, both barrows have suffered from erosion and other damage. One is 11 metres in diameter and stands 0.5 metres in height while the other barrow is 13 metres in diameter and 0.6 metres in height. Both barrows have depressions or pits at their centres suggesting that at some point they have been excavated. This probably occurred during the Victorian period when being an antiquarian was a popular hobby among the gentry. There is no record of what was found during the excavations.

The junction with the rough track with the first round barrow being seen on the left surrounded by the tufts of long grass.

Left, the first round barrow showing the central excavation pit and, right, the second barrow with a sheep salt lick tray on top.

6. Ignore the side-track down into the valley and continue along the main track. After 300 metres, and again on the left side of the track, you'll pass a large earth mound, another prehistoric burial mound. **GR 502 919.**

This round barrow is similar to the two previous round barrows just passed except for its level of preservation. The barrow is much larger than the two previous examples, being 19 metres in diameter and 1.9 metres in height. The size of the barrow makes it very prominent within the landscape as does its degree of preservation. Barrows are often surrounded by a ditch or in some cases two or more concentric ditches. With this barrow, unlike the previous two, the surrounding ditch can be clearly seen. As with the other two barrows, this one has also been excavated and, again, there are no records of any finds.

The round barrow and its surrounding ditch. Inset, left, detail of the surrounding ditch and right, the mutilated top of the barrow.

Continue along the track which undulates a little as it goes round the heads of three small valleys that feed into Thorodale. Eventually, the track finally climbs over the last rise and starts to head down to the western edge of the moor where it passes between some old quarry workings and arrives at the side of the track that forms the Cleveland Way and the Hambleton Drove Road. **GR 491 923.**

7. This junction was passed on the outward leg of the walk and if you look to the left you can see the gate through which you passed and in the near distance, the crossroads that you arrived at when you climbed up from Kepwick. Turn left to go through the gate and head up to the crossroads and its marker post. **GR 489 915.**

8. At the crossroads, turn right to go through the gate onto the tarmac road and then follow the road down the escarpment and back into Kepwick to the car park.

The waters of Gormire Lake and, inset, the lake seen from the escarpment. Walk 7: Boltby and Gormire Lake.

WALK 7: BOLTBY AND GORMIRE LAKE

The west side of the Hambleton Hills is formed by a long escarpment along the top of which runs the Cleveland Way. On the stretch that goes north from Sutton Bank, this provides some outstanding views out over the Vale of Mowbray to the distant reaches of the Pennines.

This walk follows this stretch of the popular long distance trail, discovering some of the hidden secrets from the history of this range of hills. A descent down to the village of Boltby then leads to a low level walk through fields and woods, passing Gormire Lake on the way. There are many tales about this lake and not all of them pleasant. If you believe in the walking dead then be careful, you may see more than you bargain for.

DISTANCE: 7.1 miles / 11.3 km.
ASCENT: 1,060 feet / 323 metres.
TERRAIN: The outward route follows the Cleveland Way along the western edge of the Hambleton Hills and is a fairly easy walk. The route then descends to the village of Boltby which lies below the hills, before returning by field path to Gormire Lake. There then follows a long, and in places steep, climb back up Sutton Bank to the visitor centre.
START: The National Park visitor centre at Sutton Bank. GR SE 516 831 .
TIME: 4 to 4½ hours.
ACCESS: The route is all on public rights of way.
DOGS: As the route is all on public rights of way, then dogs are allowed but please keep them under close control, preferably on a lead. You may want to keep them on a lead anyway as you go along the edge of the escarpment as in places there are cliffs and steep drops. Sheep and cattle will be encountered in some of the fields on the return leg.

GRID REFERENCES

Sutton Bank	516 831
Path junction	507 838
Path junction	508 840
Path junction	510 842
Path junction	510 849
Path junction	507 854
Boltby Scar Hill Fort	506 857
High Barn	507 867
Path/track junction	501 866

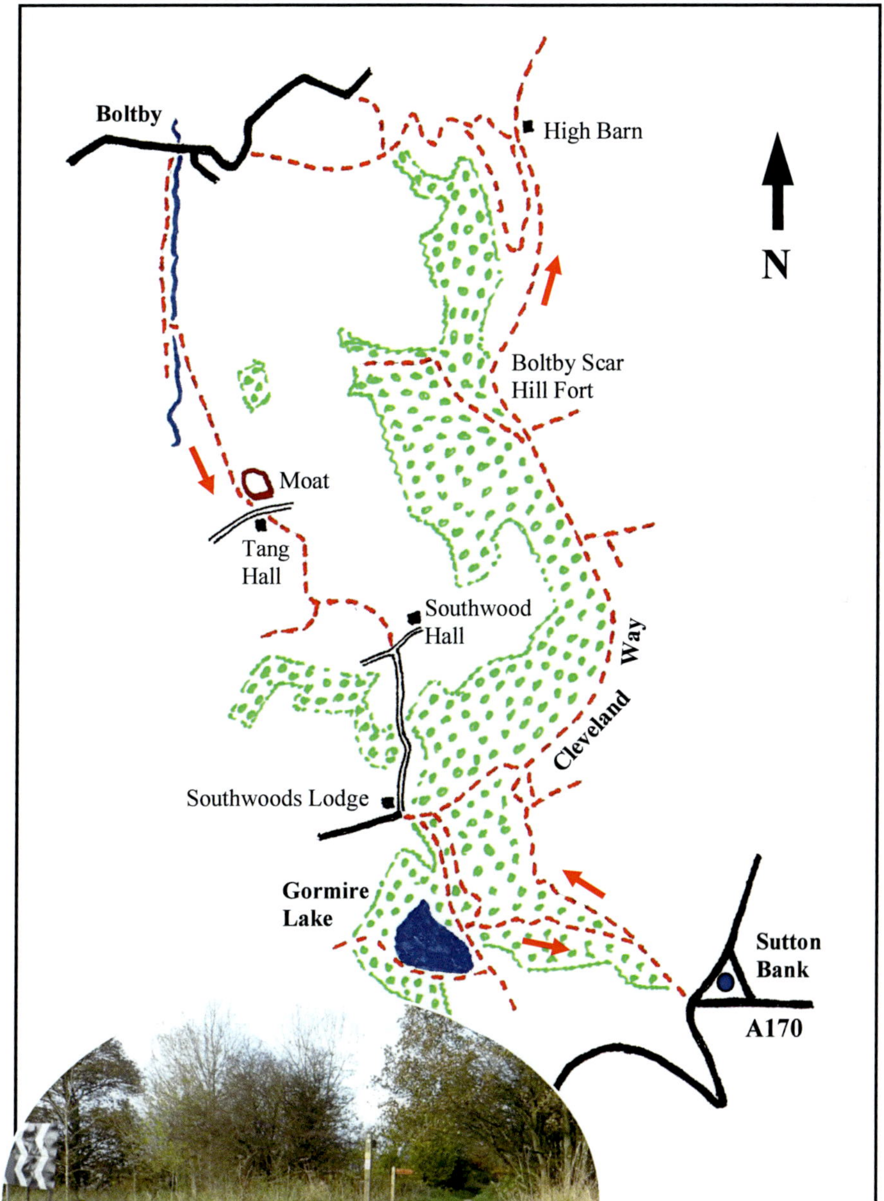

The start of the walk, at the entrance to the Cleveland Way at Sutton Bank.

Path/road junction	495 866
Road/path junction	491 866
Footbridge	492 858
Moat	494 852
Track junction	495 850
Path junction	500 847
Track crossroads	502 843
Track/lane junction	502 838
Path junction	504 833
Path junction	512 832
Sutton Bank	516 831

FGS GRADING

Grading is T6 [D1, N1, T1, R1, H2]

Distance	**1**	6 – 12 miles
Navigation	**1**	Basic navigation skills needed
Terrain	**1**	50 – 75% on graded track or path, 25 – 50% off track
Remoteness	**1**	Countryside in fairly close proximity to habitation – at least 80% of the route within 2 miles
Height	**2**	Over 125 ft per mile

THE WALK

1. From the car park at the visitor centre, go over to the top of Sutton Bank where the Cleveland Way crosses the main A170 road. Here you'll find a Cleveland Way signpost showing the way to Sneck Yate three miles away. Follow the path to the edge of the escarpment and there, it turns to follow the escarpment, heading roughly north and passing a viewing platform.

Continue along the path passing a junction on the right that has a signpost that proudly proclaims the way to the finest view in England. Stay on the path as it runs along the escarpment edge and ignore any turnings on the right for the mountain bikes. After a little while you'll pass a junction on the left with the nature trail that goes down into Garbutt Woods and which is the way that you'll come back up at the end of the walk. Continue straight ahead following the Cleveland Way.

After several hundred metres you'll pass a set of gallops over on the right, the Hambleton Hills have a long history of horse racing. Not long after that you'll come to a junction with a footpath that goes off to Dialstone Farm over on the right. **GR 507 838.**

The Hambleton Hills have been associated with horse racing for centuries and during the 1600's one of England's major races was held over the turf of these hills. Known as the Hambleton Royal Gold Cup, the race enjoyed royal patronage and attracted huge crowds. It was held over a distance of four miles and was open to horses of 5 years or younger. The race was run at the Hambletons until 1776 when, on alternative years, it started being held at the Knavesmire in York. The accessibility of the York course meant that it gradually became the more popular venue and, eventually, by the mid-1800's the Gold Cup was being held solely at York.

Incidentally, apart from the gallops, one reminder of the Hambleton's racing past still remains in the name of Dialstone Farm. A Dialstone was part of the scales that were used to weigh the jockeys, the dial telling the weight.

The gallops and, inset, some of the inhabitants of the fields.

2. Continue to follow the Cleveland Way, passing an information board for Garbutt Wood nature reserve. Not long after that, both the escarpment and the path turn to the right and you pass another junction. Stay on the Cleveland Way to Sneck Yate to come to yet another junction, this time with a bridleway on the left that goes to Thirlby Bank. **GR 508 840.**

3. Remain on the Cleveland Way and after a couple of hundred metres you'll pass yet another junction with a bridleway on the left. **GR 510 842.** Continue straight ahead as both the escarpment and the path now turn to the left and after a while come to another marker post. This one is on the right with a bridleway going off to the Hambleton Road. **GR 510 849.**

4. Not long after this junction, you'll come to another, this time a bridleway on the left going down to Boltby. Here the Cleveland Way climbs up to the next junction which is only 50/60 metres away and goes off to the right. **GR 507 854.**

5. The path now starts a climb up to the promontory and when you get to the top, you'll pass through the scant remains of the Iron Age Boltby Scar hill fort. **GR 506 857.**

In Walk 1 the route passed the earthworks that surrounded the ancient hill fort on Roulston Scar. Here at Boltby Scar a second hill fort existed within the same time frame, the Iron Age, as that on Roulston Scar. The probability is that the two were connected probably belonging to the same tribe.

However, the site itself has been used since the earliest times. Excavations on the site in 2009, 2011 and 2012 found both Neolithic and Bronze Age pottery as well as Bronze Age round barrows within the fort. This means that some form of occupation of the site could go back over 6,000 years.

Unfortunately, despite the fort being a scheduled monument, during the 1960's

The embankment of the old hill fort.

most of the earth ramparts were levelled to make the surrounding fields. Not much of the ramparts now remain and even less is accessible, just the embankments that the footpath crosses over.

6. Continue following the path as it now runs above the cliffs of Boltby Scar and as it does so, passes a junction with another bridleway on the right. You'll soon come to a small gate, go through to follow the wall on the left which separates you from the old quarry workings on the other side and once past the workings come to another gate.

Go through and continue straight ahead to the buildings of High Barn. When you get there, you'll find on your left a signpost marking a junction of paths. **GR 507 867.**

Heading for High Barn and, inset, the junction of paths.

7. Here turn left to leave the Cleveland Way and follow the bridleway down the front of the escarpment. The path heads down to a marker post and here turns left to go down a sunken track and come to a waymarked gate. Pass through and the path now bears right to go over to the fence which it now follows downhill to a marker post. Turn left here to follow the sunken lane down to another marker post.

The post now directs you right and, passing another post that directs you straight ahead, continue to come to the side of a track. Here yet another marker post directs you left to follow the track downhill where you will come to the side of a well-made vehicle track with a gate on your left. **GR 501 866.**

8. Go through the gate and then immediately turn right to leave the track and follow the fence downhill, keeping it on your right. At the bottom of the hill, cross the footbridge in front of you and continue straight ahead keeping to the left of the line of trees to come to a second footbridge. Once across this, continue straight ahead on the green path that goes steeply up the hill in front to a stile that leads onto the side of a road. **GR 495 866.**

9. Cross the stile and then turn left to follow the road round the bend and descend into the village of Boltby. As you go through the village, the footpath on the left side of the road crosses an old, hump-backed stone bridge and on the other side comes to a footpath marker post. **GR 491 866.**

An attractive village nestling in a valley at the foot of the Hambleton Hills, Boltby has its origins in the period between 867 and 954 when northern England was ruled by the Viking invader. The original settlement probably being settled by Danes in the years following Halfdan leading the Danish army northwards into what was then part of the kingdom of Northumbria.

The name of the village comes from two Scandinavian elements, Bolt a personal name and byr meaning a homestead or settlement. The name meaning the settlement belonging to Bolt. It was recorded in the Domesday Book as Boltebi.

The small, hump-backed bridge over the Gurtof Beck is an example of an old packhorse bridge. The bridge now being a grade II listed building.

The old packhorse bridge in Boltby.

10. Once on the other side of the bridge, turn left to leave the road and go down a short lane and then through the two gates at the end. The path now follows the Gurtof Beck, over on the left, and goes through five fields. In the fifth field ignore the farm bridge on the left and continue to the stile at the end of the field to cross into the sixth field. Then 100 metres after crossing into this field, you'll come to a footbridge on the left. **GR 492 858.**

11. Turn left to cross the bridge and then turn right to a gate and stile. Go through and follow the left side of the beck, going past a pipe bridge, and then bear slightly left away from the beck to a waymarked gate that leads onto a slab bridge over a stream.

Once over, cross the next field bearing to the left to follow the treeline and at the end of the field come to a waymarked gate and stile. Cross and continue following the left-hand hedge and when you get to the end of this field, go through the gap into the next where you continue straight ahead to another gate and stile. As you'll notice, this is a little bit of a strange configuration, so go through the gate first and then over the stile. Once over, look over the fence on the left to see the remains of the moat that once surrounded the manor house of the ancient vill of Ravensthorpe. **GR 494 852.**

During the Middle Ages a village named Ravensthorpe existed close to this field. The village itself has long since disappeared. However, on the other side of the fence lies a wide, deep ditch. This was the moat that surrounded the manor house of the village, the home of the lord of the manor. Although like the village, the manor house no longer exists, the moat still lies as a very prominent earthwork. This side of it follows the fence for the full length of the field, just stopping before it gets to Tang Hall.

Left, the ditch as you look over the fence and, right, the moat as you get close to Tang Hall.

12. Continue following the left-hand fence, with the moat on the other side, to the end of the field. Here go through the gate onto a very short lane to get to a second gate that leads onto a track next to Tang Hall Farm. **GR 495 850.**

13. Turn left to go past the buildings and come to a gate in front with a bridleway marker on it. However, don't go through it but instead turn right to a second gate, again with a bridleway marker on it, that you maybe didn't see at first. Go through the gate and follow the rough track. As you approach the end of the field the track turns to the left and here leave it to continue straight ahead to a waymarked double-gate, one gate after the other.

Once through the gates, follow the fence on the right down to the next gate, go through and continue down to the corner of the field where you'll find a marker post. Turn left here to continue following the fence and, within a few metres, ignore and go past the small pedestrian gate on the right and still with the fence on your right descend down to an unmarked gateway. The gatepost has a 'Beware of the bull' sign on it but there was no beast in the field on the day of the test walk. When you are through the gate, follow the path up to a fence corner where you will find another marker post. **GR 500 847.**

14. Ignore the footpath on the left and follow the bridleway alongside the fence, keeping the fence on your left. You'll pass a gate with 'Private' signs on and within a short distance come to a second gate, this one with a signpost. Continue straight ahead, past the gate, following the bridleway to Gormire Lake. At the end of the field, you'll come to a gate that leads onto a track crossroads next to the entrance to Southwoods Hall. **GR 502 843.**

15. Once through the gate, go straight ahead following the track through a waymarked gateway. The track slowly starts to climb but soon levels out. Follow the track to come to Southwoods Lodge and go through a gate next to the building onto the top of a tarmac lane. **GR 502 838.**

16. Turn left following the marker post for Gormire Lake and within a couple of metres you'll enter the woods where, after 50 metres, you'll come to a junction with a marker post. Turn right here to follow the path through the woods and after 300 metres you'll start to pass Gormire Lake.

GORMIRE LAKE.

Set amongst the trees of Garbutt Wood, Gormire Lake is one of the few natural lakes in Yorkshire. Created as a result of glacial activity, unlike most lakes it has no feeder streams but instead is fed by drainage from the surrounding land. According to tradition the lake is said to be bottomless and also hides a lost village in its depths. It is also the resting place of the undead !

During the Middle Ages there was a commonly held belief that the dead could rise and walk among the living. This was not in the modern sense of the brain-eating zombie but rather that the dead just got up and went about their everyday business. Obviously this was pretty disconcerting to family and friends left behind.

During the 1400's the Rector of Kirkby died and being a man of the cloth his body was buried at Byland. Unfortunately he was a man who would not lie down and his body took regular nightly walks through the area. The locals were obviously not over-joyed by having a walking dead man in their midst and protestations were subsequently made to the Abbot of Byland.

However, it was not until, on one of his nightly walks, he visited his concubine and caused her injury that anything was decided to be done about the matter. Even in life the rector can't have obeyed the strict religious practices of the church in order to have a concubine in the first place. Anyway, this was the last

The path alongside the lake.

straw and the Abbot had the rector's body dug up from his grave and thrown into the watery depths of Gormire Lake where he is to this day.

How much of this old tale is true is not known, apart from the belief that the dead could walk that is. Did the Abbot really have the reactor's body thrown in the lake and, if so, does the rector still take his nightly strolls only now in the woods surrounding the lake.

Initially the path is a little distance from the lake but the two soon converge so that you end up close to the shore of this natural lake. Soon after this you'll come to a junction with a path on the left with a signpost indicating a permissive path leading to the nature trail and going back to the visitor centre. **GR 504 833.**

17. Turn left here to leave the lake and start the steady climb back up Sutton Bank. Not too long after starting the climb you'll come to a junction and here ignore the left branch that goes to Southwoods and bear right to continue the climb uphill. In places the climb is quite steep but eventually as you get higher it levels out and starts to go across the slope of the hill rather than straight up it. Eventually you'll come to the top of the escarpment where you'll re-join the Cleveland Way. **GR 512 832.**

Climbing Up through Garbutt Woods back to the Visitor Centre.

18. Turn right here to retrace your steps along the Cleveland Way, back to the top of Sutton Bank and the visitor centre.

Following the path at the side of the fields leading to Studfold.
Walk 8: Studfold and Pry Rigg Plantation.

WALK 8: STUDFOLD AND PRY RIGG PLANTATION

The village of Ampleforth sits along the southern boundary of the North York Moors National Park. To the north lies the southern fringes of the Hambleton Hills while to the south of the village, the countryside becomes more gentle as it merges into the rolling Howardian Hills. This walk starts from Ampleforth and heads north, climbing out of the village to cross the farmland that covers the southern edge of the Hambletons before passing the prehistoric monument of Studfold Ring and entering the Forestry Commission woodland of Pry Rigg Plantation. As with many of the walks on the edge of this range of hills, the walk is dominated by the views across the distant landscape, in this case the Vales of Pickering and York.

DISTANCE: 6 miles / 9.6 km.
ASCENT: 928 feet / 283 metres.
TERRAIN: The route consists of field and woodland paths and tracks, there is one short road section. The stretch through Pry Rigg Plantation may be muddy in bad weather and the winter months. At both the start and end of the walk you go up and down a steep bank but other than that all of the climbs are gradual.
START: The telephone box in the centre of Ampleforth. GR SE 582 787. There is ample on-street parking on the road within the village but be considerate and don't inconvenience the locals.
TIME: 3½ to 4 hours.
ACCESS: The route is all on public rights of way apart from a small section through Pry Rigg Plantation which is on Forestry Commission access land.
DOGS: Dogs are allowed on the footpaths that make up the majority of this walk. They are also allowed through the Forestry Commission's access land at Pry Rigg Plantation although you are asked to keep them on a lead. Although most of the farm land is arable there are still a number of fields where you will encounter livestock (sheep). There are also a number of tall stiles where you may have to help your dog over.

GRID REFERENCES

Telephone box	582 787
Gate and stile	581 795
Drive/road junction	583 800
Path/track junction	587 801
Path/track junction	589 802
Track junction	590 807
Holly Bower	597 810

Photos. Top, the lane between the houses as you head away from the phone box at the start of the walk. Bottom, the stile at the end of the drive that heads up the bank into the open country.

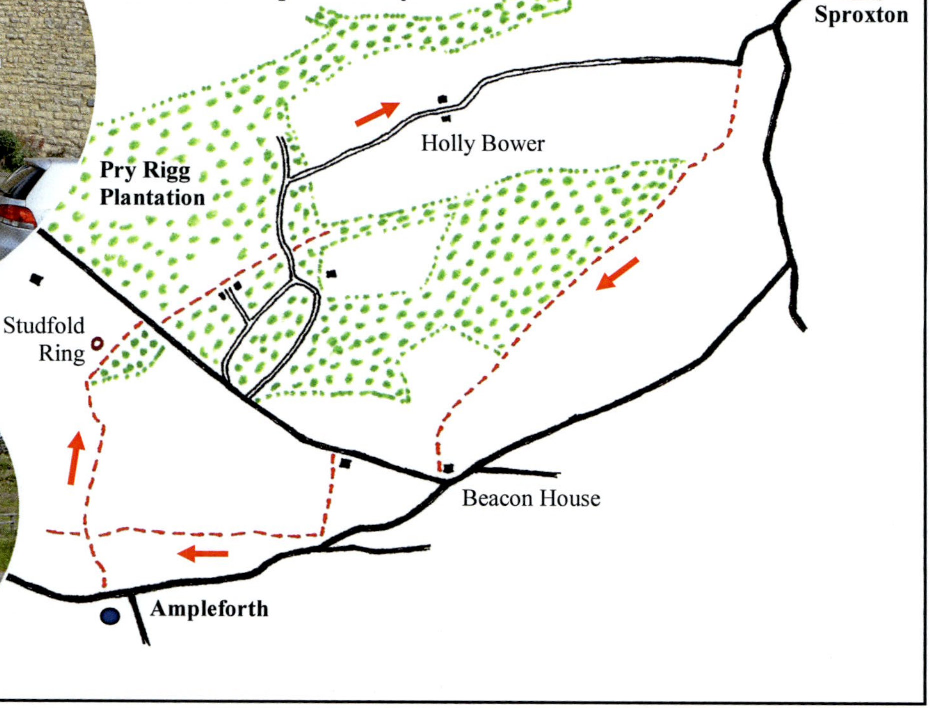

Road/path junction	611 813
Path/road junction	597 793
Road/path junction	592 794
Path crossroads	581 790
Telephone box	582 787

FGS GRADING

Grading is T6 [D1, N1, T1, R1, H2]

Distance	**1**	6 – 12 miles
Navigation	**1**	Basic navigation skills needed
Terrain	**1**	50 – 75% on graded track or path, 25 – 50% off track
Remoteness	**1**	Countryside in fairly close proximity to habitation – at least 80% of the route within 2 miles
Height	**2**	Over 125 ft per mile

THE WALK

1. From the telephone box in the centre of the village, head up the lane on the opposite side of the road. A footpath marker post stands close to the phone box pointing up this lane.

Follow the lane between the cottages and then through the large metal gates onto what is obviously a private drive but which is also a public right of way. Stay on the drive as it heads uphill and then bears left to come to a junction. Here, turn left to go through a waymarked gate to a second junction just a few metres away where you turn right to continue going uphill passing to the left of the houses.

Once past them, the drive turns right but here leave it to continue straight ahead over the waymarked stile in front and up the steep bank to join a grass track. Turn left to follow the track for a few metres to come to a crossroads of paths.

Ignore both the stile on the left and the path on the right to continue straight ahead through the waymarked gate and then the second gate. Continue straight ahead, passing the small wooden stable block, to come to a waymarked gate and stile.

Go through and, following the waymarker, continue ahead but bearing slightly to the right to come to a waymarked gate in the field corner. Once through, follow the fence on the right to come to another waymarked gate and stile. **GR 581 795.**

2. Cross the stile onto a little bit of an enclosed grass track and turn left to the next gate but just in front of it, come to a waymarked pedestrian gate on the right. Turn right through this and then follow the hedge on the left. At the end of the field, you'll come to a marker post.

The waymarked pedestrian gate on the right.

Here turn right to follow the edge of the field with the wood on your right. As you follow the edge of the wood, a short distance away on the left lies the prehistoric monument of Studfold Ring.

Within the wood, some newly-built holiday lodges become visible and not long after that, you'll come to a stile that takes you onto the access drive for the lodges. Cross and continue straight ahead down the drive to come to the side of a road. **GR 583 800.**

3. Turn right and follow the road for approximately 100 metres to come to the entrance to a Forestry Commission path on the left-side of the road that leads into Pry Rigg Plantation. Follow the path straight ahead, ignoring any side-

STUDFOLD RING

Studfold Ring stands in the field on the left, a short distance away from the path. Unfortunately there is no right of access and the path is the closest that you can get to this ancient monument.

The Ring is an earthwork enclosure that consists of an inner ditch with an outer bank. It's purpose is not totally understood, it is thought to be possibly a henge-style monument or alternatively a late Bronze Age or early Iron Age enclosure to hold animals. The earthworks had been restored at some point during the medieval period which makes it difficult to ascertain it's original purpose. However, investigation of nearby burial barrows have been carbon-dated to 700 BC and the Ring is likely to be of the same vintage.

When first built, the Ring would have been situated on a high-level plateau with full all-round visibility, the trees of the surrounding woodland tends to interrupt the view nowadays. The monument consists of a strong ditch, which in places is still four feet deep, which is then surrounded by a high bank; both the ditch and the bank are steep-sided and there is evidence that the bank may have had a stone revetment or lining. Within the ditch lies a flat area of 1.25 acres which is accessed via a single 5 metre wide entrance in the eastern side that crosses the ditch on a causeway.

At some point during the medieval period, possibly the early 1300's during the Scottish raids, the Ring's embankment has been restored with the whole monument being used as a horse corral. It is thought that the current name of Studfold comes from this period referring to a horse-fold where the mares with young foals were "falded".

Studfold Ring is a scheduled ancient monument.

Following the path through the plantation and, inset, the entrance to Pry Rigg Plantation.

paths, as it goes deeper into the woods. After a while you'll come to a junction with a track on the right and some buildings. **GR 587 801.**

4. Continue straight ahead passing to the left of the buildings. The path has become fainter now but is still easily discernible. Eventually you'll come to the side of a well-made track. **GR 589 802.**

5. Turn left to follow the track as it goes downhill, it then bends to the right before starting to climb again. After approximately 500 metres you'll come to a junction with a track on the right with a public bridleway signpost on the left of the junction. **GR 590 807.**

6. Turn right to follow the track as it heads out of the woods, through a gateway and into the fields. Stay with the track as it now slowly descends down to Holly Bower farm which can be seen in the near distance. Pass through the gateway in front of the farm to enter its yard. **GR 597 810.**

Heading down to the farm of Holly Bower.

7. Continue straight ahead between the buildings onto the farm's access track and follow, still going slowly downhill. Just over half-way down the bank, you'll pass a lonely bridleway post pointing up the track behind you, continue straight ahead.

It may seem a bit odd to have a bridleway sign half-way up this tarmac track especially as it is obvious that there are no other ways to go. However, local councils have a legal duty to place a sign at those points where a public right of way leaves a public road and this spot marks the point where the public road, coming up the bank, ends and then continues as a private track albeit with a public bridleway running up it.

As you get towards the bottom of the bank, you may be able to see a road in front dependent upon whether there are any cars going past. However, before you get there the road turns sharply left. Here, on the right-hand side of the corner is a gate, a stile and a footpath marker post. **GR 611 813.**

8. Turn right here to leave the road and cross the stile. Once over, pass the tree in front to a second stile. Cross and immediately turn right to follow the fence, keeping it on your right. The fence goes over a low rise and then into a shallow dip to come to a waymarked stile.

Cross and turn right for a few metres to the end of the field and here, ignoring the gate in front, go through the left-hand gate to head up the bank following the side of the wood. When the fence on the left ends, continue following the edge of the field, with the wood on your right, to come to a waymarked stile.

Cross and now continue to follow the path along the edge of the next four fields, always with the wood on your right. At the end of the fourth field, you'll come to a waymarked stile and here the woods on the right end.

Again, cross the stile and continue straight ahead over the middle of the next two fields on a distinctive path between the crops. At the end of the second field, you'll come to a waymarked stile, cross and turn left to follow the edge of the field round to Beacon House. When you get to the house, ignore the gate in front and turn right to follow the outside of the fence round the house to come to a gate and stile leading onto the road. **GR 597 793.**

9. Turn right to follow the road for 500 metres, going past Windmill House. Just

Following the path across the middle of the two fields.

after the house and between the end of the hawthorn trees and an electricity pole is an unwaymarked stile on the left of the road. **GR 592 794.**

The unmarked stile on the left of the road.

10. Turn left to leave the road and cross the stile. Follow the left-hand hedge as the path starts to head steeply downhill and comes to a waymarked gate. Go through and continue straight ahead down to a second waymarked gate, this one leading onto an enclosed path, which in summer may be a bit overgrown. Follow this path to the bottom of the field where you'll find a waymarked stile on the right.

Turn right to cross and then go across the bottom of the field, keeping the fence on your left, to come to a waymarked stile. Cross and continue along the edge of the field to come to a gateway. Pass through and, again, continue along the field edge, passing as you do the top of a track, to come to another gateway.

Go through and this time as you walk along the edge of the field, you'll pass a marker post before you come to a waymarked stile. Cross and then go up a little bank to continue straight ahead to a waymarked gate.

Again, pass through and continue straight ahead to a waymarked stile. Cross and continue straight ahead, going over a rough track, to come to another stile. Cross this and continue to follow the left-hand fence to come to yet another stile, this time in the bottom fence. Cross and continue to follow the fence which is now on your right. After a short distance you'll come back to the same crossroads of paths that you encountered towards the start of the walk. **GR 581 790.**

11. Turn left to follow the grass track downhill for a few metres to come to a marker post that directs you right, off the track and down the steep bank to a waymarked stile. Cross onto the drive of the houses and go straight ahead downhill to a junction. Here, turn left through a set of waymarked gates to a second junction. This time turn right and follow the drive as it continues downhill to arrive in the centre of the village, opposite the telephone box.

The trig point on the summit of Black Hambleton and, inset, the Cycle Route 65 marker post in Boltby Forest.
Walk 9: Black Hambleton.

WALK 9: BLACK HAMBLETON

Any walking guide based on a range of hills should, whenever possible, contain a walk going up to the highest point of those hills. This book is no exception with this walk which visits the summit of Black Hambleton, the top that gives its name to this range of hills.

The hills, in turn, give their name to the Hambleton Drove Road, an ancient routeway along the edge of the hills. Sections of this old road are used on some of the other walks in this book but this walk utilises the longest section which, coincidentally, is also used as part of the Cleveland Way.

DISTANCE: 8.1 miles / 12.9 km.
ASCENT: 1,178 feet / 359 metres.
TERRAIN: The majority of this route is on moorland and forest tracks with a section on field paths. There is a road section of just over 2 km on quiet country lanes and the access road to Silton Forest. There are no particularly steep climbs on this walk but there are two long and steady climbs, one from the start up to Black Hambleton and the other through Silton Forest. These two climbs give virtually all of the height gain on this walk.
START: Square Corner parking space above Osmotherley on the Osmotherley to Hawnby road. GR SE 480 959.
TIME: 4 to 4½ hours.
ACCESS: The route is all on public rights of way.
DOGS: As the route is on public rights of way, then dogs are allowed. However, be aware that the fields leading down from the moors and surrounding Nab Farm always contain cattle, often with young calves.

GRID REFERENCES

Square Corner	480 959
Track/path junction	479 944
Black Hambleton	481 946
White Gill Head	491 932
Track junction	491 928
Track junction	491 923
Track/path junction	490 919
Nab Farm	476 921
Track/road junction	469 918
Road junction	460 924
Road junction	460 926

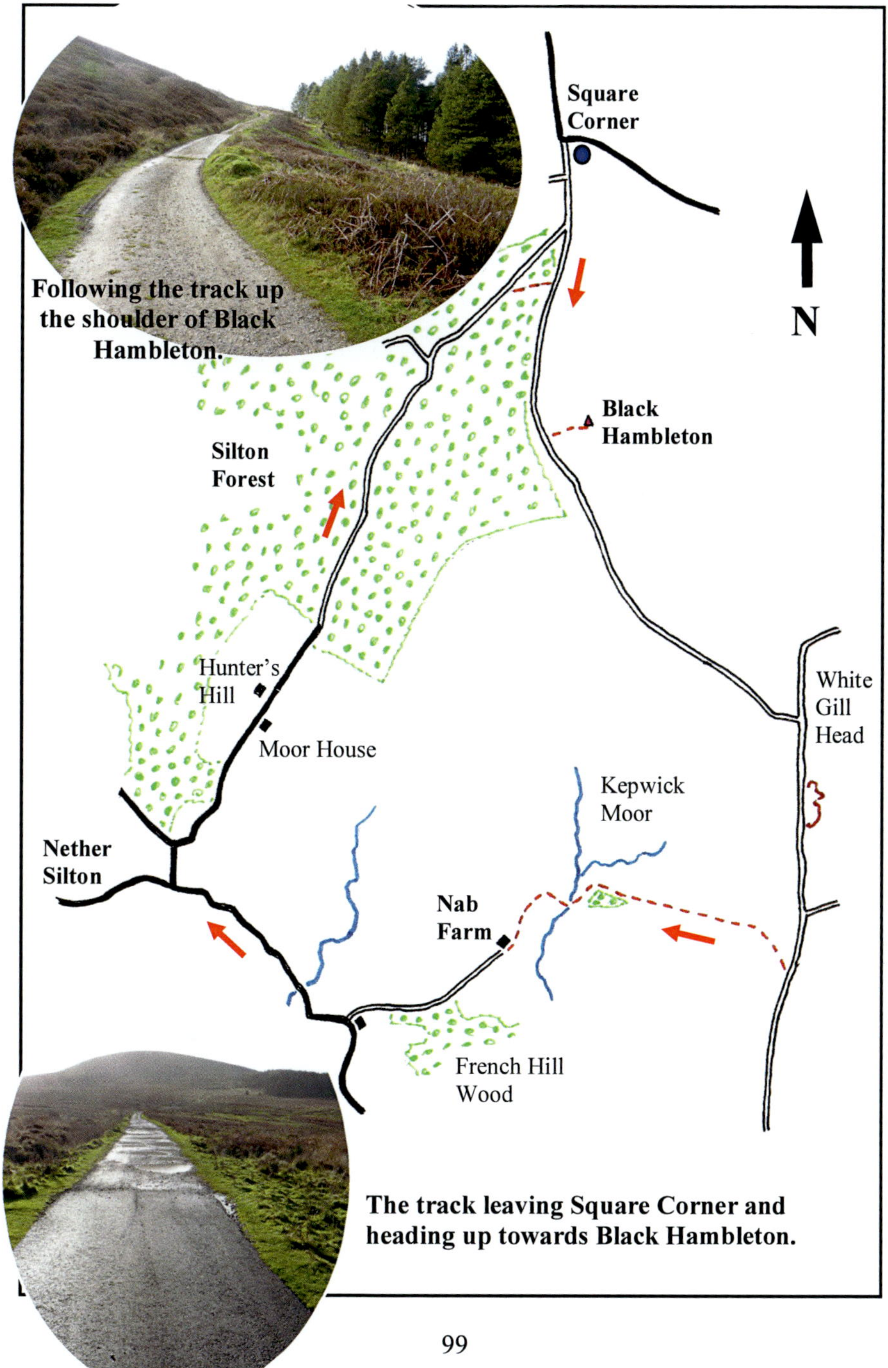

Following the track up the shoulder of Black Hambleton.

The track leaving Square Corner and heading up towards Black Hambleton.

Silton Forest	467 937
Track junction	469 941
Track junction	471 945
Track junction	472 947
Track/bridleway junction	476 951
Track junction	480 954
Square Corner	480 959

FGS GRADING

Grading is F5 [D1, N1, T0, R1, H2]

Distance	**1**	6 – 12 miles
Navigation	**1**	Basic navigation skills needed
Terrain	**0**	75% + on graded track or path
Remoteness	**1**	Countryside in fairly close proximity to habitation – at least 80% of the route within 2 miles
Height	**2**	Over 125 ft per mile

THE WALK

1. From the parking space, head up the track towards Black Hambleton, sign-posted Cleveland Way - Sneck Yate 6 miles. As you get close to the gate you'll pass the Cray Hall Stone on the left of the track. You'll then pass a track on the right before arriving at the gate.

The Cray Hall Stone is a little bit of a mystery. It was discovered laid in the heather a couple of decades ago and was subsequently erected on the spot where it was found. The mystery being, where is Cray Hall ? There is no such location locally and a search of the County archives at Northallerton at the request of the discoverer also failed to find any place with this name.

Go through the gate and continue straight ahead, starting the climb up the shoulder of the hill passing as you do, the entrance to Silton Forest. There is a long climb now up the track, the higher you get the more extensive the views over Silton Forest and the Vale of Mowbray. When you do finally get to the top of the climb you'll find a cairn on the left side of the track marking a path that goes off on that side. **GR 479 944.**

2. Turn left here to leave the track and follow the path across the heather. After a couple of metres the path widens, continue on across the moor to come to the trig point on the top of Black Hambleton. **GR 481 946.**

Standing at 1,312 feet (399 metres), Black Hambleton is the highest and most northerly of the Hambleton Hills. It is also the summit from which the range of hills take their name.

The name Hambleton comes from the Old English "hamel" meaning maimed in the sense of scarred or injured plus the word "dun" meaning hill, the Scarred Hill. As most of this range of hills have flat tops as opposed to a distinctive peak then this may have led to them being considered maimed.

3. Return the short distance back to the track and once there, turn left to continue following the track along the side of the escarpment. Eventually, after just over 1½ km, the track descends slightly, turns to the left and comes to a junction of tracks at White Gill Head. **GR 491 932.**

4. Bear right to go through a gateway that you can see 50 metres away and then continue along the track. After a short while you'll pass a track on the left that goes into some old quarries (**GR 491 928**). Continue straight ahead and after several hundred metres you'll come to another junction on the left, this one being waymarked. **GR 491 923.**

Pass the turning to go ahead through the gate which is a short distance in front. The track now starts to descend into a dip between the hills and when you get to the bottom of it you'll find a waymarked gate in the wall on the right. **GR 490 919.**

5. Turn right to go through the gate and then follow the left-hand wall as it starts to head downhill. Stay on the green track that runs close to the wall and after a long descent you'll pass to the right of a clump of trees.

Following the wall down into the valley.

At the bottom of these trees the path joins a track which you follow as it bears round to the left and comes to a waymarked gate.

Go through this gate and head down the bank before turning right to cross Old Gill and then follow the track up the other side of the valley heading towards Nab Farm. Once at the farm, follow the waymarker through the yard to the left of the barns and then through the gate onto the access track. **GR 476 921.**

6. Follow the access track straight ahead towards French Hill Wood. When you are alongside the wood, the track bears right and then descends to join the side of a road next to Cross Lodge. **GR 469 918.**

7. Turn right to follow the road which shortly after joining goes round a right-hand bend. The road then crosses a bridge over the Sorrow Beck and starts to climb. After 800 metres the road comes to a junction on the right which is sign-posted as part of Cycle Route 65. **GR 460 924.**

8. Here turn right to head towards Rose Cottage which lies a short distance in front of you and just after passing the cottage come to another road junction on the right, this one with a Dead End sign and another for Cycle Route 65. **GR 460 926.**

The road junction after Rose Cottage.

9. Turn right and follow the road as it climbs up past another house. When you get to the top of the bank, the road starts to descend as it heads up the valley of the Sorrow Beck towards Silton Forest. The road goes up the valley for 1 km passing Moor House on the right and then Hunter's Hill on the left. The road then starts to climb and shortly enters Silton Forest. **GR 467 937.**

10. The road now becomes a track, continue straight ahead going to the right of the forest sign and then, within a few metres, go round the gate following the markers for Cycle Route 65. The track now starts a steady climb and after a few hundred metres passes a junction on the right with an old stone building and a large, cast metal cycle way marker post on the corner. **GR 469 941.**

Heading up through Silton Forest.

Continue straight ahead, climbing quite steadily now and after a while you'll pass a rough track going off to the left (**GR 471 945**). The main track continues uphill on a long climb, as it gets near to the top you'll come to a track junction on the left (**GR 472 947**).

Pass the junction and shortly after, the track turns to the left and starts to level out. A little while after you'll come to a bridleway signpost on the right side of the track (**GR 476 951**). Stay on the track as it now starts to go downhill to ultimately go through a gate and come to the side of the track that you followed at the start of the walk to go up the shoulder of Black Hambleton. **GR 480 954.**

11. Turn left and head downhill back to the car park which can be seen a short distance away.

THE HAMBLETON DROVE ROAD

The Drove Road, also shown as Hambleton Street, Hambleton Road, Cleveland Road and High Lane at various points on the OS map, is an ancient routeway across the hills of the western escarpment of the moors. The use of the route may even date back to the prehistoric, there are certainly enough relics along its length that date back to the Bronze Age and the earlier Neolithic.

From a point near Yarm where it crossed the River Tees, the road climbs the Cleveland Hills at Scarth Nick to cross Osmotherley Moor and then runs along the ridge above Cod Beck reservoir, past Chequers and Square Corner and up the shoulder of Black Hambleton. Continuing across Little Moor by Steeple Cross, High Paradise and Sneck Yate, it reaches the top of Sutton Bank at Cooper Cross before continuing it's long course southward via Scotch Corner, Old Stead and Coxwold.

The Drove Road leading up from Square Corner.

Prehistory ended with the invasion of the Romans and the start of their written history. In many parts of the country ancient routeways were continued to be used by the Romans, albeit the old tracks were replaced by Roman roads. There is no evidence of this happening with the Hambleton Road although the routeway seems to have continued being used, possibly by only the native people, well into the Dark Ages and beyond.

After the Norman invasion there is a tradition that William the Conqueror and his armies used the road during the Harrying of the North in 1069 when the northern counties were put to sword and flame in response to a rebellion by the

English nobles. By 1246 the route was being described as the 'Regalis Via', the King's Way, within documents in the Rievaulx Chartulary and the road was enjoying royal protection.

From the end of the 16th century up until the late 1800's, it became one of a network of routes that were used to bring Scottish cattle down from the Highlands to the lucrative meat markets of the industrialised towns of England. In the days before refrigeration, meat was transported while it was still on the hoof and thousands of cattle, mainly Galloway and West Highland, walked down from Scotland. Travelling in vast herds the average pace was two miles per hour covering between fourteen and sixteen miles a day. The advantage of using this relatively high level route was that it avoided the toll roads that crossed the more populated and agricultural lands of the Vales of Mowbray and York.

Although the heyday of the Drove Road was during the 17th and 18th centuries it was also during this period that it received an alternative name. After the cattle had been sold in the southern markets, the drover then had to walk back home along the Drove Road laden with the proceeds of the sale to pass to his employers. Now he had to contend with the constant threat of robbery as he strode out along the Thieves Highway ....

The Drove Road running along the edge of the escarpment after Black Hambleton.

Nowadays sections of the route are modern roads tarmaced over, while others are stony tracks and still others long stretches of soft springy grass. With the Road running the length of the Hambleton Hills it is perhaps inevitable that some of the walks in this book will utilise sections of it at some point during their length.

APPENDIX

Ferguson Grading System (`FGS`)

1. Introduction
The FGS has been adopted as a means of assessing the nature and severity of the various walks in this book and the abilities and equipment needed to tackle each one safely. The FGS was developed by Stuart Ferguson, a long time fell and trail runner, climber, mountaineer, mountain-biker and general outdoor enthusiast. In the opinion of Trailguides the FGS is the most accurate and comprehensive grading system for comparing off-road walking, running and mountain-biking routes anywhere in the country.

2. The System
Tables 1 & 2, set out below, are used in order to give a grading to each route. Table 1 sets out three categories of country that a route could potentially cross, together with a range of factors that would need to be considered when tackling that route. The three categories are, Trail, Fell and Mountain, and after assessing which category best fits the route, a letter, either `T`, `F` or `M`, is allocated to that route. Where a route does not fit perfectly into one of the three categories the closest category is allocated.

Table 2 deals with five specific aspects of the route namely distance, navigation, terrain, remoteness and height gain, and each one is allocated a letter, `D`, `N`, `T`, `R`, and `H`. Each letter is also given a severity score from the range 0-3 or 0-4, in respect of distance (`D`). The higher the number, the more severe the route. The five severity scores are then added together to give an overall score. The overall score is then put with the Table 1 category letter (i.e. `T`, `F` or `M`).

In order to show how the grading has been determined for each walk in this book, the five individual severity scores are set out, in square brackets, immediately after the actual grading. So, for example, Walk 4 The Eastern Dales has a grading of T5 [D1, N1, T0, R1, H2], indicating that it is a Trail Category walk with a total severity score of 5. This is made up of the five specific severity scores, for distance (`D`), navigation (`N`), terrain (`T`), remoteness (`R`) and height gain (`H`), of 1, 1, 0, 1 and 2 respectively. The highest total severity score which can be achieved is 16 and the lowest total severity score achievable is 0.

The table which accompanies the grading at the start of each walk sets out the specific factors, extracted from Table 2, that need to be considered when tackling that particular walk.

TABLE 1

	TRAIL	FELL	MOUNTAIN
Description	Lowland and forest areas including urban, cultivated and forested locations.	Moorlands and upland areas which may include some upland cultivated and forestry areas plus possibly remote locations.	Upland and mountain areas including remote and isolated locations.
Height	Not usually above 1,000 feet but may go up to 2,500 feet	Usually above 1,000 feet, up to 2,500 feet and above.	Usually above 2,500 feet and up to 4,000 feet.
Way-marking	Usually	Limited	None
Terrain	Usually graded paths, tracks and trails but may include some off-trail	May include some graded paths, tracks and trails but mainly off-trail	Virtually all off-trail
Height gain	Limited height gain	May include considerable height gain	May include some severe height gain.
Effects of weather	Very limited effect	May be prone to sudden weather changes	Extreme weather a possibility
Navigational skills	None to basic	Basic to competent	Competent to expert
Equipment	Walking shoes/boots. Possibly waterproofs Food and drink dependant upon route.	3/4 season walking boots. Full waterproof cover. Possibly map and compass dependant upon route. Food and drink dependant upon route.	Mountain boots. Full waterproof cover. Map and compass. Food and drink
Escape Routes	Yes	Some	Some to nil

TABLE 2

Score	**0**	**1**	**2**	**3**	**4**
Distance	Up to 6 miles	6 – 12 miles	12 – 18 miles	18 miles +	24 miles +
Navigation	No navigation skills needed	Basic navigation skills needed	Competent navigation skills needed	Expert navigation skills needed	
Terrain	75% + on graded track or path	50 – 75% on graded track or path 25 – 50% off track	25 -50% on graded track or path 50 – 75% off track	Under 25% on graded track or path Over 75% off track	
Remoteness	Urban	Countryside in fairly close proximity to habitation – at least 80% of the route within 2 miles	Countryside not in close proximity to habitation – less than 20% of the route within 2 miles	Remote, isolated location	
Height gain	Less than 100 ft per mile	Over 100 ft per mile	Over 125 ft per mile	Over 250 ft per mile	

Notes to Table 1

Graded paths = Well established paths with a stable surface.

Escape routes = The opportunity to cut the route short and return to the start without completing the full course in the event of weather changes or unforeseen incidents.

The Author

Keven Shevels

Kev has been involved with outdoor sports since his school days when participation in the Duke of Edinburgh award revealed the beauties of hill and dale and resulted in him walking or running through the countryside of the North East and beyond for most of the last forty years. Many of these trips into the great outdoors being visits to the heather-clad uplands of the North York Moors, an area for which he has developed a great fondness.

Over the last six years, Kev has put pen to paper describing routes through the North Pennines that reveal his passion for both the countryside and the history that has shaped it and the people who live upon it. That, coupled with an in-built curiosity to go and view things that spark his interest, tend to result in routes that take the reader into new, undiscovered areas and reveal a history that may not be apparent from the outside. He is not ashamed to admit that he is one of these boring people who can sit and spend hours reading a map like more normal people read a book. His great delight is coming up with new routes that he can subsequently explore and investigate. All of this has resulted in an easy to read, informative style of guidebook that has proved very popular among the walking fraternity and received very favourable reviews in both local and national press.

Now Kev returns to one of his favourite areas, the North York Moors, and in this, the third in a number of books that he is planning on the Moors, he explores that area of upland that frames the south-western edge of the Moors, the Hambleton Hills.

The author having a break out in the Durham countryside.

WALKING NORTH EAST

Walking North East is the brand name for the walking publications produced by Trailguides and reflects the pride that we, as North Easterners, have in our countryside, our history and our culture. Based in Darlington, we are a small independent publisher specialising in guidebooks centred on the North Eastern counties of England. Our target is to produce guides that are as user-friendly, easy to use and provide as much information as possible and all in an easily readable format. In essence to increase the enjoyment of the user and to showcase the very best of the great North Eastern countryside. Our series of books explores the heritage of us all and lets you see your region with new eyes, these books are written to not just take you on a walk but to investigate, explore and understand the objects, places and history that has shaped not just the countryside but also the people of this corner of England.

If you've enjoyed following the routes in this guide and want news and details of other publications that are being developed under the Walking North East label then look at the company website at **www.trailguides.co.uk**

Comments and, yes, criticisms, are always welcomed especially if you discover a change to a route. Contact us by email through the website or by post at Trailguides Limited, 35 Carmel Road South, Darlington, Co Durham DL3 8DQ.

Other walking books from Walking North East.

NORTH YORKSHIRE.

Currently available.

Walking the Hills of Upper Swaledale.
Walks Around Gunnerside.
Walks around Reeth & Upper Swaledale.
Walking around Osmotherley and the Cleveland Hills.
Walking in the Hambleton Hills.

Coming soon.

Walking in Arkengarthdale.
Walking in Wensleydale.
Walking in the Cleveland Hills.

COUNTY DURHAM.

Currently available.

Hamsterley Forest.
Ancient Stones.
Mid-Teesdale Walks.
Walking in Teesdale.
The Barningham Trail.
Walks from Stanhope.
Walking in Weardale.

Coming soon.

Walking in Weardale Book 2.
Walking the High Hills of Teesdale.

NORTHUMBERLAND.

Currently available.

The Cheviot Hills.
The Hills of Upper Coquetdale.
Walks Around Rothbury and Coquetdale.
Walks on the Wild Side: The Cheviot Hills.
Walking in the Allendales.
Walks from Wooler.
Walks from Kirknewton.
Walks in Hadrian's Wall Country.

Coming soon.

Walking in the Simonside Hills.
Walking around Hexham and Corbridge.

Have a look at our Facebook page - **Walking North East** for current news on ourselves and our publications. The page also contains news, views and articles on all aspects of walking within the North Eastern counties of Cleveland, Durham, Northumberland and North Yorkshire. Definitely well worth a look and clicking the Like button.

For those that don't have or want to use Facebook then why not subscribe to our monthly newsletter. Titled 'Walking North East' this contains the same news, views and articles as our Facebook page. Subscriptions are free with no obligation to purchase and can be made via our website at www.trailguides.co.uk . Previous issues of Walking North East can also be accessed free via the website.

Disclaimer

The information contained in these pages and the route descriptions is provided in good faith, but no warranty is made for its accuracy. The contents are, at the time of writing and to the best of our knowledge, up-to-date and correct. However, the world is a changing environment and what is correct one day may not be so the next. Care should always be taken when following these route descriptions just as it should when following maps or waymarkers of any kind..

No guarantee whatsoever is provided by the author and/or Trailguides Limited and no liability is accepted for any loss, damage or injury of any kind resulting from the use of this book, nor as a result of any defect or inaccuracy in it.

As with all outdoor activities, you and you alone are responsible for your safety and well being.